M BERKELEY

It Came
from
Berkeley

Berkeley

How Berkeley Changed the World

Dave Weinstein

GIBBS SMITH
TO ENRICH AND INSPIRE HUMANKIND
Salt Lake City | Charleston | Santa Fe | Santa Barbara

First Edition
12 11 10 09 08   5 4 3 2 1

Text © 2008 Dave Weinstein
Cover image postcard published by R. & C.
Hakanson. Courtesy Sarah Wikander.

Published by
Gibbs Smith
P.O. Box 667
Layton, Utah 84041

1-800.835.4993 orders
www.gibbs-smith.com

Designed and produced by Kurt Wahlner
Printed and bound in China

Library of Congress Cataloging-in-Publication
Data
Weinstein, Dave.
It came from Berkeley : how Berkeley changed the
world / Dave Weinstein. – 1st ed. p. cm.
ISBN-13: 978-1-4236-0254-5
ISBN-10: 1-4236-0254-4
1. Berkeley (Calif.)–History–Anecdotes. 2.
University of California, Berkeley–History–
Anecdotes. I. Title.
F869.B5W45 2008
979.4'67–dc22

2008013969

To my wife, Mary Barkey, for listening to story after story about Berkeley

Acknowledgments

Thanks to Paul Grunland, Ken Duffy, Daniella Thompson, and Steve Finacom for your editing and historical advice; Susan Snyder, David Farrell, and the staff at the University of California, Berkeley's Bancroft Library; Ken Cardwell, John Aronovici, John Underhill, Phil Gale, and Mark Peters at the Berkeley Historical Society; Stacey Zwald and Adam Nilsen at the Oakland Museum; Aaron Brody of the Pacific School of Religion; Nick Robinson at the university's Institute for Governmental Studies; Anthony Bruce at the Berkeley Architectural Heritage Association; Sarah Wikander for her postcards; Brenda Montano of the East Bay Regional Park District; and the staff at the Berkeley Public Library. Also, thanks to Michiko Uchida and Kim Cranney.

Contents

Introduction

How Berkeley Changed the World

Some people argue that Berkeley is not part of the world at all but a place apart, an island floating off America's "Left Coast." But take a closer look. Has there ever been a town more all-American? One more optimistic? More progressive? More representative of America at its liberal best—or occasionally, its worst?

Do Americans believe in individualism, living the good life, and participatory democracy? That's what Berkeley is all about. And has there ever been a city in America in which religion and spirituality have more effectively served as forces for social change?

This book suggests that, rather than existing outside of America, Berkeley exists at its heart. From its early years—thanks to its professors, its forward-thinking police chief, its citizens who fought for public parks—Berkeley has pioneered much of what is best about America.

As the tales you are about to read show, Berkeley pioneered public university education, temperance as a force for families, and the spiritual in art. Throughout its history, Berkeley's leading thinkers have defined the good life not as a life of wealth but as a life devoted to the arts and the betterment of their fellow men and women.

Berkeley pioneered humane crime fighting, decried corporal punishment of children, helped create national parks, and helped invent the concept of regional open space.

During the 1960s, when the world at large woke up to Berkeley's influence, young people associated with the university defined free speech as a cause and helped give America a true counterculture. Throughout the troubles of the Sixties, Berkeleyans fought for people's power, helping change America from a country where local governing was largely run by a tight-knit cadre of city fathers down to one where individuals and neighborhoods hold sway.

Berkeley didn't change America in a piecemeal fashion, a bit of this and a bit of that. Berkeley changed America by becoming "Berkeley"—a place where the individual is celebrated and where no one is afraid to speak up.

This book, therefore, is a social history of the town, built around the proposition that what happened in Berkeley has had repercussions elsewhere. Berkeley is in many ways a typical American city, its birth marked by theft, chicanery, and high-minded hopes, its growth guided by wily developers, its progress hindered by natural disasters. This book tells many of those stories.

But Berkeley is also unique. What made it so? Only by understanding how Berkeley ever-so-gradually became "Berkeley" can we see how Berkeley changed America—and continues to change it. What if America as a whole were more like Berkeley?

Berkeley continues to amaze.

So how did Berkeley become Berkeley?

How did "Berkeley" the noun become "Berkeley" the adjective? And what does that adjective mean? Insanity?

The *Berkeley Courier* suspected as much back in 1905. Under the headline "Erratics in Berkeley," the paper mused: "The records of the Police department show eleven cases of insanity in four months . . . This record is larger than the combined records of the rest of the county in the same time. Can it be that this educational center affects its residents this way? Some say that it would have been an easy thing to have more than doubled the record."[1]

Historians, going back to 1878, have made much of the fact that Berkeley became a city on April Fools' Day.

"Nut Hill," as a hilly neighborhood north of campus has long been called, was settled in the early twentieth century by professors, businessmen, and Berkeley's original Bohemians—including architect Bernard Maybeck, whose eccentric houses liberally dot the area. Other residents included theater director Sam Hume and his psychiatrist wife, Portia Bell Hume, who inhabited a detailed re-creation of a medieval cloister; and Florence Treadwell Boynton and family, who lived and danced in the Temple of the Wings, a house without exterior walls.

Some historians suggest, unpoetically, that the hill was named not for its denizens but for the acorns that drop from its oaks. Others blame the name on an earlier inhabitant of the hill, Captain Richard Parks Thomas, who enjoyed shooting a cannon from the hillside every Fourth of July, or on the actual nuts that some inhabitants made a major part of their diet. To most observers, "Nut Hill" meant just what it suggests.

As the century progressed, the "insane Berkeley" theory only grew stronger—even among many Berkeleyans. "The first time I came to Berkeley I felt like a bit player in a Fellini movie," a *Daily Californian* reporter confessed in 1977.[2]

The Campanile *towers over Sproul Plaza and Wheeler Hall, no matter what influence you're under. Postcard courtesy of Sarah Wikander.*

A few years later, *Daily Cal* reporter David Pickell wondered, "Why is Berkeley always making headlines?" His answer: "Because the place is *weird*. Through the eyes of the national media, *people* don't live in Berkeley, bizarre cultural, sociological and political mutants do."[3]

"What's a circus without the clowns?" Berkeley's street poet and bubble blower, Julia Vinograd, observed of UC's Sproul Plaza in 1985.[4]

In the mid-1960s, the underground paper *Berkeley Barb* mused over the essence of Berkeley. The Roving Ratfink, an unnamed *Barb* columnist, gave readers a quiz: "Test Yourself. How Berkeley Are You?" What music do you dig, he asked. Where do you live? What do you drink? How do you party? What films, restaurants, magazines, jobs, and stores do you like?

"Actually," the Ratfink reported, providing the details, "in only three categories did there seem to be a real Berkeley answer: preference in pads (the backyard cottage wins by a length, if only because it's a Berkeley specialty), art form practiced (the typical Berkeleyan today is not writing or painting; he's making a film), and what can loosely be called politics (a Berkeleyan is pro-civil rights and anti-Vietnam war)."[5]

Fellow columnist Shea Were took a darker view of the subject. "Sometimes," he started out, "one only gets a sense of Berkeley by leaving it. Once gone, with renewed exposure to the outside world, we strikingly realize how really isolated we are from the rest of the world . . . Here, because our world is narrow and because we find people here who understand us, we get into the habit of thinking there are more of us than there really are . . . The fact is that Berkeley people are not even the majority in Berkeley."[6]

Berkeley's remarkable turn to the left in the 1960s—before that, it was largely a Republican-controlled town—added to its "People's Republic" image.

"Welcome to 'The People's Republic of Berkeley,' a reputation earned during the social upheaval of the 1960s," the *Tampa Tribune* trumpeted in 2001, right after the 9/11 attacks. "This place makes the term 'The Left Coast' more than geographical in nature," the paper wrote. The *Tribune* was laying into Berkeley because Congresswoman Barbara Lee, whose district also covers Oakland, was the only member of Congress who voted against authorizing war.[7]

Periodically, loyal Berkeleyans have protested such journalistic treatment. In the mid-1980s the *San Francisco Chronicle*'s Charles Burress fought "Berkeley Bashing." "Journalists have seriously likened Berkeleyans to Joseph Stalin, the Ayatollah Khomeini, Peter Pan and plain thugs," Burress complained.[8]

After all, most Berkeleyans, politically liberal though they be, are far from berserk. Many even have jobs, pay their bills, and enjoy living in peace.

But the attacks never stop. "On the funky streets of Berkeley, California, it's forever the '60s," the *Wall Street Journal* observed as the 1980s came to an end. "Oh, Berkeley, Berkeley, Berkeley," reporter Ken Wells gushed. "If it's true that the eccentrics of earth moved to America and the eccentrics of America to California, then the eccentrics of California have a special place in their hearts for this funkily scenic haven on the east shore of San Francisco Bay."[9]

After an encounter with a crystal seller on Telegraph Avenue ("Take it into the bathtub with you," the merchant advised) and after worrying that the city council might adopt a Palestinian refugee camp as a sister city and ban "ownership" of pets, Wells settled in for a chat with R. Howard Bloch, chair of Cal's French department and author of a satirical novel about Berkeley. "This is a town in which half the people are seeking to overthrow the federal government while the other half are seeking the perfect croissant," Bloch said.

The Gourmet Ghetto, concocted in the early 1970s by people who had burned their fingers in the political oven of the '60s, has often been served up to show that Berkeley has turned its back on its more authentic past. How little those critics know about Berkeley's authentic past!

Berkeley, in fact, has always been about living the good life and making that life available to all: not the luxurious life, not the sybaritic life, and certainly not the ostentatious life. Charles Keeler—as Berkeley a character as you can find—saw the good life as the cultured life. He wrote *The Simple Home* in 1904 to urge Berkeleyans to build modest wood-shingled dwellings among the live oaks and invented a Cosmic Religion that was all about music and poetry.

Andy Ross, the longtime owner of the fabled Cody's Books on Telegraph Avenue, revealed similar thinking a century later in his definition of Berkeley. "It's Rodeo Drive for intellectuals."[10]

Perhaps it's a sinister plot more than journalistic laziness that leads headline writers and reporters to trot out that hackneyed "People's Republic" line. By convincing readers that Berkeley is not part of the real America, they seek to render it irrelevant, something to laugh about but not think about or heed.

If so, the plot has failed. Over the years Berkeley has proven itself an All-American city in the best sense—a town that exemplifies the values of freedom, openness to new ideas, and experimentation in art, science, literature, and social practices. Berkeley has always generated ideas—and sent them forth.

Berkeley has pioneered the modern public university (with an oft-ignored promise of free education for all), free speech, neighborhood preservation, listener-supported radio, school integration, accessibility for disabled people, urban wilderness parks, the preservation of shoreline and creeks, and the rediscovery of the blues.

And Berkeley has often been a very well-run city—thanks in large part to the university, whose experts have helped the city govern itself, plan its parks and playgrounds, and guard its health.

Berkeley's "firsts"—or near-firsts—are many: the first to divest from South Africa, to create a citizen police-review panel and a tool-lending library, to provide curbside recycling, to ban Styrofoam cups, and to install curb cuts for people in wheelchairs. The university's scientific "firsts" are too numerous to mention, from the atom smasher and nuclear medicine to the invention of the wet suit.

Berkeley, in fact, is a quintessential American city. Its story is the story of many American cities. Half of it grew up around shoreline industry as the town of Ocean View, to the west. The other half developed to the east as a kind of company town, dominated by the university. The problems that hit Berkeley hit towns everywhere: too little water and too much garbage, racial discord and poverty, deindustrialization, and the dismantling of an efficient public transportation system.

The Caffe Mediterraneum *brought good espresso to Berkeley in 1957 and has served as a congenial spot for Beat poets and thinkers of all persuasions ever since. Courtesy of photographer Kim Cranney.*

Sproul Plaza *on the university's campus serves as Berkeley's town square. Courtesy of photographer Kim Cranney.*

But through it all, Berkeley has remained a special place, thanks to the university, which attracted scientists, writers, scholars, and artists; to the town's location along a Bohemian trade route that also included San Francisco, Carmel, Big Sur, and the Russian River; and to wealthy businessmen who appreciated art, architecture, music, and gracious brown-shingled living.

In the mid-twentieth century, two hard-fought battles over race—one over a proposed law banning discrimination in housing and another over school desegregation—sent many conservatives fleeing town. For a good seven years, starting in 1964 with the Free Speech Movement, anti-Vietnam War protests, Third World Liberation Front battles, and People's Park, Berkeley was often a war zone with young people rioting and police and troops teargassing, beating, occasionally shooting, and often doing their best to contain the damage.

Then in 1971, the "radicals" took over the city council. Besides blocking a shopping center at the waterfront and fighting for affirmative action, according to former councilman and opponent Tom McLaren, they "caused an exodus of longtime citizens."[11]

Is it surprising that some people left? But through it all, Berkeley established a reputation as an innovative, politically liberal, free-spirited town.

So what really makes Berkeley Berkeley?

It might surprise outsiders to hear that the answer is religion. The university had its roots in a Christian endeavor, and though it quickly became secular, many of its leaders were religious men. Berkeley was designed from the start to be an Arcadian town, quiet and pure, altogether different from the Sodom and Gomorrah across the bay.

"Berkeley enjoys an immediate moral atmosphere," the *San Francisco Call* noted in 1891, "because the law prohibits saloons within a mile of the State University. The consequence is that the churches meet with little opposition and the moral growth of the city is not retarded."[12] And the entire town went dry in 1905—a good fifteen years before the Volstead Act brought Prohibition to the nation as a whole. (Enforcement, however, was lax.)

Holy Hill, a city within a city of theological seminaries, is no anomaly. Throughout Berkeley's history, many of its progressive leaders were motivated by religious impulses—the founders of the co-ops and International House; the fighters for good government, women's suffrage, integration, and the city's progressive public health programs; the environmentalists; and many of the peace activists. Equally spiritual, if not always pious, were Berkeley artists and writers, including poet Charles Keeler and painter William Keith. And let's not forget—the university was founded by missionaries.

Berkeley has always had a puritanical streak about it—and still does. Berkeley's so-called Bohemians spent their time not in absinthe-soaked dives but in living-room salons in brown-shingled homes, the Swedenborgian Church in San Francisco, or the Unitarian Church in Berkeley.

San Francisco has been awash with strip joints and lap dance parlors for decades. But when the Mitchell Brothers opened a branch of their San Francisco porno emporium in downtown Berkeley in 1982—complete with Godzilla-bosomed Candy Samples on opening night—the town screeched. "Not surprisingly, an army of enraged, sex-negative feminists showed up and assaulted customers both verbally and physically," according to "Rugpony," who, in an Internet posting, identified himself as a neighbor of the theater. The experiment didn't last long.

Citizen activism made Berkeley an exciting, maddening place—and inspired people everywhere to get involved. The successful citizen effort to preserve the beloved Berkeley Hills in the 1930s by creating an urban park district—the first such park district in the nation—served as a nationwide model.

Berkeley has always been a town of individualists, and the fight for individual freedom, freedom of thought and action, and optimizing the individual's potential is a major theme running through the town's history. You see it in Charles Keeler's paeans to living the artistic life and in university president Wheeler's exhortations to students to think for themselves.

It's what the Free Speech Movement was all about. Student and community activists have battled the university for decades over a variety of seemingly disparate issues, ranging from foreign wars to parks to trees. Underlying all of those fights is the fight for individual self-determination.

Professor of politics Sheldon Wolin, speaking during one anti-Vietnam War rally, expressed the desire well: "What we are now witnessing is the effort of freeing ourselves from the multiversity. We are trying to become post-bureaucratic men and women."[13]

The Free Speech Movement may be Berkeley's best-known example of standing up to the powers that be—but there have been hundreds more. As Weldon Rucker, Berkeley's city manager at the start of the twenty-first century, put it, "Berkeley is a place where people come from all over the country to practice democracy."[14]

Poet Julia Vinograd, *blowing bubbles by the student union in the late 1960s, has been a Telegraph Avenue presence for decades. Photo by A. Moon. Courtesy of the Berkeley Historical Society, 4.9.4 196 2607.*

How Berkeley Was Born

How Berkeley Took to the Hills

The founders of the University of California knew they'd lucked upon the most beautiful site in the world, better than the Italian lakes and closer in spirit to the Olympian home of the gods. Poet Joaquin Miller agreed. "It sits in the lap of huge emerald hills, and in the heart of a young forest," Miller wrote in 1886, "with little mountain streams bawling and tumbling about; wild oats up to your waist in the playgrounds and walks, and a sense of largeness and strength grander than I ever felt in and about any university before."[1]

And every house built in the town's upper reaches, residents bragged, had a view through the Golden Gate. Berkeleyans could sit on their porches and watch buildings going up in San Francisco. The Berkeley Hills were wilderness. Bears roamed and salmon spawned in Strawberry Creek.

No one considering the history of Berkeley can ignore the hills—because nothing had as much effect on the city's development nor on its social and cultural life than the hills. Without the hills, Berkeley would never have become Berkeley—a town that glories in the beauty of its wilderness and in wilderness everywhere.

Berkeley became a city of hikers. Cornelius Beach Bradley described some favorite hikes in the 1898 book *A Berkeley Year.* "The quiet saunter up Strawberry Canyon, the long afternoon ramble over the hills to Orindo Park, the all-day tramp by the Fish Ranch to Redwood Canon and Maraga Peak, or more strenuous still, the cross-country trip to Diablo."[2]

Twenty years later, the lively coed Agnes Edwards headed for the hills whenever she could. "I don't think there's another place in the world where you can see so many different kinds of scenery," she wrote her folks. "The Bay is all spread out before us, the hills rise out of our yards almost, and altho' we're within an hour's distance of as citified a city as you could want, in ten minutes walk we can get so far from civilization that we'd never know we were near a city."[3]

Perhaps nothing—not Bohemianism, free speech, citizen activism, spirituality, nor good food—defines Berkeley so much as its beauty, which attracted the men who first made up the faculty and the poets, artists, architects, business people, real estate developers, and scientists who followed. In 1903, when President Teddy Roosevelt came to speak during commencement, the university's beloved president, Benjamin Ide Wheeler, invited him to gallop on horseback through the hills. Over the years, Berkeley's thinkers did their thinking

1887: *The early campus got much of its character from the wild hillside that provided more than a touch of wilderness—including bears. From Illustrated Album of Alameda County, California by Jos. Alex Colquhoun. Courtesy of the San Francisco History Center of the San Francisco Public Library.*

while walking in the hills—none more so than physicists Ernest Lawrence and Robert Oppenheimer. It was on these strolls that they hashed out details for Berkeley's biggest contribution to history, the atomic bomb.

William Keith, perhaps Berkeley's finest painter and certainly its most successful, walked every day through a forest of campus oaks on the way to the ferry and his San Francisco studio. Many of those oaks turned up later in paintings of the Sierra. The Sierra Nevada itself was no stranger to Keith. He hiked there often with his friend John Muir.[4]

Thanks to Muir, Professor Joseph Le Conte and his son, Professor Little Joe, as well as biblical scholar William Badè and other Berkeleyans who helped found the Sierra Club, the Sierra became a Berkeley outpost, with locals like Bill Colby leading trekkers on month-long stays, complete with mules and slabs of bacon.

Colby recalled one of those trips with Little Joe. "Joe bought a mule and it was black. He called it Blackie. And before he got through with his trips, that mule was white—perfectly white. Everybody said that Joe would take the mule up to the top of a pass and put his head over the edge. When the mule looked down and saw where he had to go, he got so frightened that it scared him white."[5]

Another Berkeley mountain man was artist and professor Worth Ryder, who introduced modern art to Berkeley in the 1920s, later bringing in the abstractionist Hans Hofmann. But Ryder preferred the outdoors. "There is something primordial in the joy it gives me," he wrote of the Sierra. "Standing naked and alone in the wilderness, facing the sun and the wind. And such a wind it is. Hurrying across vast untrodden spaces, ozoned by fragrant forests, and cooled by crystal ice fields. It ripples across my back like joyous laughter."[6]

Strawberry Canyon

was dotted with live oaks and chaparral when the university was young. Courtesy of the Bancroft Library of the University of California, Berkeley.

How Berkeley Remembered Its Spanish Heritage

José Domingo Peralta

Shortly after the United States entered the Second World War, Ina Rosenquist, the owner of a creekside home in Berkeley's Peralta Park neighborhood, was surprised to see an elderly lady—short, heavyset, and wearing a long black dress—stepping across her lawn toward the creek. With her were two younger men.

The woman, who was about eighty-five, was Virginia Osuna, whose father once owned the lot as well as most of what later became Berkeley. Osuna showed the men—one was historian J. N. Bowman—where her father, José Domingo Peralta, built the first house by a European ever built in Berkeley, an adobe, in 1841. Then she walked to a laurel tree overlooking Codornices Creek.

"This is it! I remember this tree well—its heart has been burnt," Osuna said. "I climbed it many times! Yes. There were other trees around too, oaks and more bay trees. This side of the creek was the stockyard where my father kept his riding horses or cattle he was ready to sell."[1]

Osuna, whose original given name was Gabriela, died shortly after the visit. It's a shame she was never interviewed more extensively, because it's from Osuna that we've learned most of what is known about her father.

Bowman, who taught at the University Extension, had been studying the Spanish presence in Berkeley at least since the early 1920s, "discovering" Monument Rock—an immense outcropping that the Peraltas used as a convenient property boundary in 1922—and doing the same for the Peralta adobe site in 1933.[2]

The story of Domingo Peralta makes clear just how typically American Berkeley was before it emerged as a city. His story was all too representative of the fate of the Californios.

Domingo, who was born in 1794, remains the most mysterious of the Peralta brothers. He was short, stocky, and dark complected like his father, Luis Maria Peralta. Courteous, friendly, and impulsive, Domingo had four children with his first wife. When she died, he remarried and sired six more.

Luis, who had been granted much of the East Bay for military service on behalf of Spain, divided his property among his sons. Domingo was asked by his father to stake out a ten-thousand-plus-acre site in the East Bay, in part to guard against trespassers. The attempt proved in vain.

Domingo chose a creekside site he'd first encountered—and named—in 1818 while exploring the property with his brother Antonio. They found and feasted on quail eggs, so named the creek *Codornices*, the Spanish word for quail.

The cattle ranch prospered. Soon Domingo moved from the adobe to a two-story wood-framed house painted a cheerful yellow, with a long porch facing west. It's worth remembering that Domingo settled on his rancho in 1841—only a few years before California passed from Mexico to the United States in 1848.

1890s: Le Conte Oak greeted visitors to the forested campus. Courtesy of the Bancroft Library of the University of California, Berkeley.

Domingo's life grew complicated, especially once the Gold Rush attracted hordes of settlers. Like most owners of Spanish or Mexican land grants, Domingo was harassed by American squatters, many of whom were more sophisticated than that term implies. Squatters soon started developing a commercial downtown—on land owned by Peralta. In 1852, only eleven years after settling along Codornices Creek, Domingo was arrested for assaulting two squatters on his property and fined $700. His sons also ran into trouble with the law, accused of stealing cattle, horses, and barley.

The tax man and the Lands Claims Commission, which sought to clarify title, also made Domingo's life hellish. The burden was on Domingo to prove his ownership, and it got expensive.

Short of cash for fines and bail, Domingo was soon selling off his land in increasingly sizable chunks. Another pox came in the form of lawyer Horace Carpentier, a legendary shyster, who stopped by to help. Osuna remembered "Horacio," whom she found "neither handsome nor ugly," riding on a white horse. "He speaks such beautiful Spanish," Domingo told his daughter. "He finally told me that if I would sign some papers, written to be sure in English, he would help me to win against the squatters, and I have signed. But I do not feel so easy about it."[3]

By the mid-1850s, Domingo's holdings—once including all of Berkeley and Albany—were down to thirty acres. He died a pauper in 1865.

Places:

The site of the Peralta adobe on Codornices Creek is marked by a historic plaque at 1302 Albina Street. The adobe and a second wood-frame house owned by the Peraltas are long gone.

How Berkeley Freed Its Slaves

Napoleon Bonaparte Byrne

By the start of the 1850s, a small community—Ocean View—was developing along Berkeley's shoreline. Former sea captain James Jacobs built a wharf at the mouth of Strawberry Creek to haul produce to San Francisco. Another man followed with a roadhouse and a grocery. J. T. Fleming, who bought Fleming Point from Peralta, ran cattle there. Contra Costa Road—today's San Pablo Avenue—had a stage line.

By 1855, the shoreline was graced with its first factory, the Pioneer Starch and Grist Mill.

Farmers were setting up shop inland. One of the first was Napoleon Bonaparte Byrne, who arrived in 1859 with his wife, four babies (the Byrnes would have four more), and two Negroes, after traveling for six months in covered wagons from Missouri, a slave state.

Byrne, who bought 827 acres in what today is North Berkeley, was convinced Berkeley was ideal farming land—at first. Others had the same idea. Soon the rolling hills were dotted with farm houses, enclosures, wheat fields, and cattle, and connected by meandering tracks.

By 1860, the Byrnes had a home. Nap's wife, Mary Tanner Byrne, was charmed. "The view is enchanting," she wrote to friends back East, adding, "Even from the city we can see our little house distinctly."[1]

Ocean View and what would later be called Berkeley were already different communities—Ocean View, industrial and working class with small workers' cottages; Berkeley, home to large landowners. But Nap and Mary would often detour through Ocean View when visiting friends in Oakland—because Contra Costa was "one of the handsomest roads in the state."

"We frequently ride down to Oakland on this road tho' it is somewhat farther than our own road," Mary wrote, "but the scenery is so beautiful that I can never look at it enough."

The Byrnes threw grand parties; their guests were "mostly of the Southern elite of Oakland."

It was from Oakland that a party of lawmen came calling shortly after the Byrnes' arrival in town to ask about their longtime servants, Hannah and Uncle Pete. Word was that the African Americans—probably Berkeley's first black residents—were slaves. California was a free state.

The Byrnes denied it; so did Hannah and Uncle Pete. Nonetheless, they were "freed" and taken away. According to the Byrne's granddaughter Marguerite C. Hussey, both Hannah

1890s: Napoleon Bonaparte Byrne in retirement. Courtesy of the Berkeley Historical Society, 4.9.3.190 2005, 4.9.3.190 2005.

and Pete quickly returned.[2] By 1867, Hannah had dropped out of sight, but Uncle Pete, who did well in the whitewashing business, remained friends with the Byrnes and visited frequently. On one visit, Hussey said, a neighborhood kid yelled out, "Here comes Nigger Pete." Pete was hurt but unabashed. "California white trash," he observed.

Droughts made farming difficult in Berkeley. So in 1871, Byrne bought Venice Island, fifty miles east on the San Joaquin River, hoping to turn a river delta into rich farmland. He soon had five hundred Chinese laborers building levees and piling tules for a bonfire. "Mr. Byrne thinks as great fortunes will be made there with Chinese labor raising wheat as ever were made in Southern plantations," Mary wrote.

But levees kept breaking, the tules were too wet to burn, and the Byrnes were soon selling off their Berkeley property to support Venice Island. "We are having a wet time up here," Mary wrote their son Peter in 1874. "I only wish I could offer congratulations in a more substantial manner," she wrote him later on his graduation. "But alas! We have nothing here to spare but water."[3]

The Byrnes returned to Berkeley in 1880 and rented a house while Byrne tried the coal and firewood business. He later became popular as the town's postmaster.

Places

Congregation Beth El, 1301 Oxford Street, occupies the site of the Byrne homestead.

How Berkeley
Founded a University

Historians have argued over who founded the University of California. But two questions are easier to answer—Who put his life on the line for it? And not once but twice?

When Henry Durant, a minister and scholar from Massachusetts, arrived in San Francisco in 1853, proponents of a college—missionaries, really, dispatched to the California wilderness—had already been at work for four years. Samuel H. Willey, a Congregationalist minister sent to Monterey in 1849 by the American Homes Missionary Society, hoped to establish a Christian nonsectarian school to provide the first higher education in the new state.

The religious roots of what would become the University of California are worth noting because Berkeley has remained a remarkably high-minded place. It is that very high-mindedness, often verging on self-righteousness, that has made Berkeley such an inspiring town.

Willey made several trips back East to raise funds but had little luck. "The feeling in the east was that it was absurd to send money to California, the place that gold came from," wrote Millicent Washburn Shinn, an early Cal graduate who became deeply involved with university affairs.[1]

1890s: Commencement beneath the oaks. Courtesy of the Bancroft Library of the University of California, Berkeley.

It was not until Durant arrived in California—thirty-seven days after he arrived, to be exact—that the new institution held any classes. He opened the Contra Costa Academy, a "college school for boys," in rented quarters in Oakland with three students. It almost closed immediately. As recounted in 1901 by William Carey Jones, Cal's first law professor and a university historian, the first crisis came when the school couldn't pay the building's manager, Mr. Quinn, who decided to turn the place into a bar and lodging house. Durant tried to stop him.

"He got into a rage," Durant recounted, "laid his hands on me with considerable force, and was

1860s: Henry Durant, a founder of the university and, later, mayor of Oakland. Courtesy of the Bancroft Library of the University of California, Berkeley.

1960: Left to right: Regent Donald McLaughlin, Governor Pat Brown, and university president Clark Kerr mark the university's one hundredth anniversary at Founders Rock. It was here in 1860 that the campus was dedicated and then in 1866 named in honor of George Berkeley— Bishop of Cloyne and the Anglo-Irish philosopher and educator who wrote the poem that includes, "Westward the course of empire takes its way." Berkeley was talking about civilization shifting toward the Pacific—not about imperialism. Courtesy of the Bancroft Library of the University of California, Berkeley.

The inscription on the plaque reads:

FOUNDERS' ROCK
COLLEGE OF CALIFORNIA
APRIL 16.1860

INSCRIBED MAY 9,1896

North Hall, California University, Berkeley, Calif.

1870s: North Hall, one of the two original university buildings. Postcard courtesy of Sarah Wikander.

pushing me away, when suddenly he became as pale as a cloth, lifted his head and began to pray. He prayed that I would pray for him that God would have mercy on his soul. His religion came to my relief."

The second incident, as recounted by Durant, goes like this:

Construction was underway on a new building when the funds ran out. Durant worried that the contractors would take possession in lieu of pay. "I came over at night, took a man with me, went into the house, put a table, chairs, etc., into one of the rooms upstairs, and went to bed." Next morning, as predicted, the contractor arrived with "two burly fellows."

"I had no means of defense except an axe that was under the bed," Durant said. Durant warned that if they proceeded into the room, "you will not only commit a trespass upon my property, but you will do violence upon my body."[2]

"That seemed to stagger them and finally they left me in possession."[3]

In 1855, the Contra Costa Academy became the private College of California and quickly sought a rural location. By 1857, it began acquiring farmland in the foothills north of Oakland. The college was transformed into a state university in 1868, taking advantage of the federal Morrill Act, which provided support for states that organized colleges to teach agriculture and the mechanical arts. The university had taken on a dual identity—liberal arts and the classics, and practical training.

The first classes in Berkeley, at North and South halls, started in 1873.

How Berkeley Developed a Cow Town

Hannah and Uncle Pete may not have been Berkeley's only slaves. Wilhelmine Bolsted Cianciarulo, who moved to Ocean View (today, West Berkeley) as a child in 1883, stated in a memoir years later that the owners of the community's main gathering place, Sisterna Hall, "had one Indian slave named Pedro. He slept in the barn with the horses and was in demand at all times until he died."[1]

The Bolsteds lived in a "country garden home" at Fourth Street and Allston Way, a few blocks from Captain Thomas's soap factory. The manager had a two-story Victorian with gar-

dens and a Chinese cook. White workers had three-room cottages. The Chinese lived in shacks—but they impressed the young girl nonetheless.

"Chinese women and children dressed very elegantly, when they went to San Francisco to visit friends or relatives or to do their necessary shopping," she wrote.

Also nearby were two slaughterhouses on University Avenue. "The screams of the poor beasts could be heard three

1910: Two boys, two "plugs," one donkey, c. 1910, with Berkeley bungalows making their mark in the hills. Courtesy of the Berkeley Historical Society, 4.9.7.191 7232.

blocks away," Wilhelmine remembered. "Neighbors were thankful when a law was passed that stopped this custom."

The neighborhood was a work-in-progress, with "a beautiful beach of white sand" past Second Street, flour and grist mills hugging the shore alongside Indian shellmounds, scattered

1900s:

Among the industries that grew up around the shoreline in Ocean View was the Standard Soap Company. Courtesy of the Bancroft Library of the University of California, Berkeley.

1900s:

Much of central Berkeley was rangeland in the early 1900s. These teams were working near the present intersection of Sacramento and Cedar streets. Courtesy of the Berkeley Historical Society, 5.1.7.190 5873.

housing, wagon trails, and elevated wooden sidewalks that washed away during storms.

Wilhelmine's father worked for the Spreckels sugar company in San Francisco, and part of his pay was in sugar. She fed it to neighborhood horses, which she learned to break so they could haul wagons. For added cash, the Bolsteds raised chickens and Wilhemine sold the eggs in San Francisco. And Mr. Hirshfeld, who ran a grocery on the ground floor of Sisterna Hall, was kind enough to accept eggs as currency. "Money was scarce those days," Wilhelmine wrote. "Most people had little bags of gold dust or nuggets saved somewhere."

Wilhelmine, who later taught at Thousand Oaks School, played the organ and directed the choir at two of Berkeley's earliest churches, Westminster Presbyterian and Good Shepherd. Wilhelmine was so talented, she often found herself onstage for the weekly Saturday night party at Sisterna Hall.

"I remember being sound asleep in bed and wakened up to go to sing and play for the crowd because sometimes the talent they expected had not arrived by ten o'clock and they just couldn't keep the audience waiting any longer," she wrote. "My parents did not like it but everybody had to be a 'good fellow' or it would just be too bad for you if you ever needed any help."

Nothing impressed young Wilhelmine more than the cowboys from nearby ranches, who, dressed in blue jeans during the week, "looked quite disreputable."

"On Saturday nights they came to Sisterna Hall dressed to kill. Custom-made suits with new chaps, fancy flannel shirts, bright silk ties, and wonderful big hats with elegant hat bands were worn."

"Could they ride horses? Oh yes! They would run alongside and jump in the saddle and both rider and horse would whirl around a half a dozen times and off they would go with a yell, like a streak of lightning."

How Berkeley's University Students Got the Spirit

For a university that lacked ivy-covered walls, famed alumni, a gym, or much in the way of equipment, the University of California had high standards.

To gain admittance, high school graduates needed to show mastery of "higher arithmetic . . . including the extraction of square and cube roots . . . Algebra, to Quadratic Equations; Geometry, first four books . . . English grammar, Rhetoric, Geography, and History of the United States." For the College of Letters, students would be tested on Latin Grammar, Caesar, Virgil's "Eclogues," "Georgics" and six books of the "Aeneid"; Cicero, Xenophon and the "Iliad." And for literary pursuits, candidates needed "an elementary acquaintance with some modern language."[1]

The living was far from easy. Most students and faculty lived in Oakland in the early years, and the commute by horse-drawn streetcar could take an hour. Going to college was a big deal, and parents often moved to town along with their children.

Once a small commercial strip developed at the Telegraph Avenue entry to campus, students complained that the French restaurant was too expensive. Berkeley quickly got its first "coffee saloon," however.

On the positive side, tuition was free for California residents and, "so far as possible," the university promised that "students who desire to earn something by their manual labor will be employed upon the ground."[2] From the start, the university

DELTA UPSILON ROUGH HOUSE CA 1900 BERKELEY

1900: *The men of Delta Upsilon. Courtesy of the Bancroft Library of the University of California, Berkeley.*

pioneered the idea that education should be free and available to as many young people as possible.

In 1873, the year classes started at the Berkeley campus, President Daniel Coit Gilman oversaw twelve professors, seven instructors, and three chemistry assistants. Some of these proved to be remarkable men, including "the two Le Contes," Joseph in geology and his brother John in physics.[3] Like a number of other early professors, the Le Contes were refugees from the South, who were driven away by Reconstruction and found job offers lacking from higher-prestige schools in the East.

It didn't help that faculty pay was poor. "Apparently there is a great dearth of able men in the country who are anxious to serve their country at $3,000 a year," the *Occident*, a student paper, reported in 1882.[4]

Though professors may have gone to Berkeley for lack of better offers, many loved the area and thrived. Berkeley's setting, especially its hills, provided much of the appeal for many, along with the town's proximity to the High Sierra. Berkeley was already becoming a center of the nascent environmental movement. John Le Conte became University of California president. Joseph became a pioneering mountaineer, a friend of John Muir, and a founder of the Sierra Club.

Students too were entranced—so much so they'd break into song. "The groves and hills are forever echoing to the dulcet

1907: The annual freshman-sophomore brawl started in 1907 with tugs of war and other competitions that sometimes got out of hand. Courtesy of the Bancroft Library of the University of California, Berkeley.

tones of Seniors, Juniors, Sophs and Freshies," the Blue and Gold yearbook reported that first year, "each of whom imagines he possesses a God-given knowledge of time and tune."[5]

Could town and gown conflicts be far off?

"The cold nights are not sufficient to dampen the spirits of the students whose songs may be heard way into the small hours as they patrol the streets," the Berkeley Advocate reported a few years later. "Some of the residents of the town are frequently annoyed by the impossibility of sleep during the time which the caroling bands spend in their vicinity."[6]

Singing wasn't the worst of it. For fun, students would occasionally storm a vaudeville theater or flood roadways by opening water tanks alongside rail tracks. The worst offenders, according to the Occident, which proclaimed itself an "anti-fraternity" paper, were the frat men—especially the men of Chi Phi.

"The worst to be urged against the fraternity is the dissipated character of its members," the paper editorialized in 1882, citing one man who returned from San Francisco one night accompanied by "several disreputable girls." The editorial continued: "Then this representative of fraternity culture, this true and upright gentleman, introduced one of the girls as his sister."[7]

The early years saw the birth of solid Bear traditions—including adoption of the campus mascot, the Golden Bear, who was a real bear in the early years. There was the Big C built on Charter Hill above campus and the annual Burial of "Bourdon" and "Minto"—two unpopular freshman texts, complete with a parade carrying the books inside a coffin, a bonfire,

Places

One of the two original buildings, South Hall still stands by the Campanile. It is all that remains of the old Victorian campus that was superseded by architect John Galen Howard's ode to the classics.

much drinking afterwards (a "bust"), and, at least once, a threat of gunplay.

"How the Sophomores tried to steal everything they could get their hands on and how they didn't do it," is how the Occident headlined its story on the 1882 fracas. It began with the arrival of the event's key speaker at Berkeley Station. "As soon as he stepped off the train they made a rush for him. What they would have done with him is an unsolved mystery, for he pulled a pistol on them and ordered them to stand off."[8]

How Berkeley's Coeds Doffed Their Hats

Unlike many of the nation's universities, Cal admitted women almost from its founding, starting in 1870, and without restriction. Women were beginning to attend colleges in large numbers at this time, but not every institution was as welcoming as Cal. Its great rival in the Bay Area, Stanford, began limiting coeds by a strict quota in 1899. By 1892, graduate Millicent Washburn Shinn, the first woman to earn a PhD at Cal, reported in the magazine Overland Monthly that women made up one-third of the student body.

Berkeley may have pioneered education for women, but coeds weren't always well treated. When Lilian Bridgman appeared on campus in 1886, a top graduate of Kansas State, she knocked on the door of Joseph Le Conte, whose reputation brought her there. He got her set, and soon Lilian was

c. 1900: *Women students in black "plugs"—battered top hats typically worn by junior men. Hats designed for women tended to be broader brimmed. Courtesy of the Bancroft Library of the University of California, Berkeley.*

scuttling through creeks for her master's thesis, "The Origin of Sex in Freshwater Algae." She was stymied, however, by one professor who refused to put his "valuable compound microscope in the hands of any coed."[1]

Coming to her rescue was Phoebe Apperson Hearst, whose late husband, George, made millions in the Nevada silver mines. Phoebe, one of the university's greatest benefactors, specialized in the care of coeds. With Hearst's funding, Lilian bought a microscope. Mrs. Ellen Metcalf McHenry—whose daughter Mary McHenry Keith would become Berkeley's leading suffragist—let Lilian use her greenhouse as a lab.

Places

Hearst Avenue is named for Phoebe Apperson Hearst, not for her husband and not for her son, newspaperman William Randolph Hearst. Julia Morgan's impressive Berkeley City Club, built in 1929 as the Berkeley Women's City Club, shows the civic stature women had attained.

Two decades later women still weren't seen as campus equals. Men were scandalized in 1904 when coeds proposed cheering at the Big Game with Stanford. But sophomore Alice Joy insisted that women do the traditional Oski Wow Wow cheer. "I firmly believe that future games will see the women taking just as active a part in the cheerleading as the men do now," Alice predicted.[2]

Three months later an even greater scandal shook the town. "Coeds will wear no hats on campus," the *Courier* blared. It started when a math professor complained about "women who insisted on wearing big picture bonnets and sitting in the front of the room to the exclusion of the vision of the men students, who usually sit in the back."[3]

By March, a call to doff hats by the Associated Women Students had succeeded beyond their dreams. More than 4,000 girls in Berkeley had "joined the hatless brigade."

"The power of example is strong," the *Courier* reported. "Now almost the entire younger female population of Berkeley has followed suit." "Society misses," high school students, "even the tots in the primary classes scorn a hat." "To the stranger, the custom is somewhat astonishing, but its picturesqueness cannot be questioned." The hatmakers, of course, were "absolutely threatened with bankruptcy."[4]

Perhaps it was the hat crusade, perhaps not, but by August 1905, the *Courier* reported, more women than men were signing up for the new term. "They make good learners and they are the rank and file of the teaching class of the state," the paper applauded. "More power to them!"[5]

How Berkeley Communicated by Sign

The School for the Deaf and Blind

It's not surprising that Warring Wilkinson succeeded at teaching deaf and blind students to communicate, because he was a masterful communicator himself—forceful, eloquent, and with more than a touch of show biz. "When he got up to speak before an audience," said his son-in-law, UC Extension head Leon Richardson, "you could feel his magnetism."[1]

"He was a graphic and graceful sign-maker," wrote William A. Caldwell, a teacher at the school who didn't always see eye to eye with his boss, "and it was an inspiring sight to see him put his thoughts into signs."[2]

For the public, the high point every year at the California Institute for the Education of the Deaf and Dumb, and the Blind was a pageant open to all—especially newsmen. "Blind and deaf graduates excite wonder of visitors," the *San Francisco Examiner* oohed and aahed in 1900. The pièce de résistance—"c. 1915 'long-distance' communication from deaf to blind. A deaf mute in the gallery signaled a message . . . to another

c. 1900: Warring Wilkinson. Courtesy of the Bancroft Library of the University of California, Berkeley.

THE PRIZE OF
SUPERIORITY IN
FOOTBALL WON BY
THE UNIVERSITY

1898. N°1899.

Places:

The California School for the Deaf moved to Fremont in 1980. The school in Berkeley became UC's Clark Kerr campus. Nearby Warring Street is named for Wilkinson. Tilden's The Football Players *remains a campus landmark among the oaks south of the Valley Life Sciences Building*

1900:

Douglas Tilden's The Football Players *was awarded to Cal because of victories over Stanford. Postcard courtesy of Sarah Wikander.*

mute on the platform by means of sign language. It was then communicated to a third mute by facial expression and this mute passed it on to a blind girl by the means of signs, which the latter read by touch from the deaf mute's fingers. The blind girl in turn wrote the message on Braille machine, and a blind boy read it out to the audience. The whole process took about ten seconds."[3]

But Wilkinson was more than show. "A firm believer in the inadvisability of pure oral instruction," Wilkinson also believed in integrating deaf and blind people into society.[4] One of his toughest battles was to classify the institution as a school, not an asylum. "To call a school of this kind an asylum was an injustice to the pupils and an offense to their parents and relatives," he said.[5]

Wilkinson arrived at the small school in 1865. He moved it from San Francisco to 131 acres half a mile south of the site that later became the state university. The deaf school moved to its Berkeley campus in 1873, even though the 1868 earthquake tumbled its stone buildings.

A hands-on administrator, "here, there, everywhere about the place," according to Caldwell, Wilkinson befriended his students, helped them find jobs and get into universities, and followed their progress through life.

There was much to follow. Graduates of the school first entered the University of California in 1873. Prominent businessmen, chemists, and even the city editor of a San Francisco paper got their start at the school. Granville Redmond, the deaf Los Angeles painter known for superb landscapes of poppies, came to the school in 1875 at age four. Redmond's signing was so eloquent that he became an actor, taught Charlie Chaplin mime, and played the sculptor in Chaplin's film *City Lights*.

The most prominent early graduate was Douglas Tilden, who was accepted at Cal but opted to study art in Paris. Wilkinson made sure he had the means. Tilden's statue *The*

Bear Hunt won praise, and San Francisco's mayor James Phelan became a patron, promising to give Tilden's sculpture *The Football Players* to whichever team, Cal or Stanford, could win the Big Game two years running. Cal got the statue in 1900.

Tilden's career sputtered in the twentieth century. For a decade, starting in 1915, he suffered what he called a "spell of inertia." His wife, who was also deaf, left him in 1926. When he died in 1935 in his home studio on Channing Way, "impoverished" at sixty, one paper reported, "Mallet and chisel, that had carried the eloquence of his mute genius to the world for nearly half a century, lay almost within reach of his slender hands."[6]

How Berkeley Entertained a Resort

M. B. Curtis

Real estate developers exploited Berkeley's charms from the start of the streetcar era, enticing picnickers to scenic hillside spots in hopes of selling homesites.

In 1895, plans were afoot to turn the university campus into a summertime Chautauqua, a setting for intellectual bliss. "You can wander by the hour under gnarled trees with grotesque trunks knotted with age, over rustic bridges by picturesque rocks, or rest in the shadow of the sacred halls of learning," the promoters observed.[1] And several proposals came and passed for running tramways to the top of Grizzly Peak.[2]

Berkeley's most successful resort—the Claremont Hotel—opened in 1915. Most of it is actually just across the city line in Oakland. One tale, probably true, reveals that one of its developers, John Spring, lost it in a domino game.

MR. CURTIS AS THE COMMERCIAL TRAVELLER

AS MDLLE. CÉLESTE.

MR. AND MRS. CURTIS IN "SAM'L OF POSEN."

But the Claremont's story is nowhere as interesting as that of Berkeley's least successful resort, Peralta Park.

The man behind the scheme, M. B. Curtis, emerged as one of Berkeley's first truly remarkable figures—just one of many who would give the town much of its character. He made little mark as an actor when he first appeared in New York circa 1870. He played "small comedy characters at an equally minute salary," the *New York Times* remarked in 1885, adding: "He was not regarded as a comedian of any particular value."[3] Nor was he known for a pleasing personality. The *Times* said he had trouble hiring actors, "owing to the widespread impression that nobody can get along with him."

But Curtis, who was born Mauritz Strelinger in Bohemia, was an astute businessman. Curtis acquired rights to George Jessop's "Sam'l of Posen: the Commercial Drummer" and was soon barnstorming the country with it. His company included Curtis's wife, the exotically named Albina Fleurange. By 1885, in San Francisco, Curtis was flying high with the play, "a highly popular piece about a Polish Jew," at the Alcazar Theater.[4]

The *Los Angeles Times*, which in 1886 reviewed both "Sam'l" and its sequel, "Spot Cash: or Sam'l of Posen on the Road," reported sellout crowds. Both plays, the critic wrote, were built entirely around Sam'l's amusing antics—strutting in loud clothes while pushing shoddy wares. "Sam'l of Posen" showed "an attempt at something aesthetic," the *Times* wrote.

The sequel, however, he called "about the worst trash that was ever placed before a confiding public."[5]

By 1887, Curtis was also making his mark on Berkeley, turning the area that once surrounded Domingo Peralta's adobe into what he hoped would be the grandest hotel on the West Coast. With investors, he built a sprawling Victorian palace complete with turrets and fanciful towers, which would have been the grandest building in Berkeley today had it sur-vived. He also subdivided the neighborhood and several Queen Anne–style homes were built.

Curtis lived well, his former night watchman A. D. White reported, throwing $1,000 dinners and so fattening himself that, before each new stage season, he'd bring in a prize fighter to work off fifty pounds, with "a bonus of a dollar per pound for removing flesh."[6]

"He didn't have a cent of money yet he somehow or other got that Peralta Park tract," Curtis's onetime partner George

c. 1880: Peralta Park Hotel. Postcard courtesy of Sarah Wikander.

Places

Several streets in and around Peralta Park bear curious names: Posen, Albina. Two other streets, Carlotta and Joseph, were also named for characters in the play. St. Mary's College High School occupies the site once occupied by the hotel. The Victorian home at 1330 Albina were part of Curtis's subdivision.

Schmidt recalled. "He was the greatest promoter I ever saw. He gave the biggest lunches and dinners at his home and gathered all kinds of wealthy people from San Francisco there. When he finished feeding them they were ready to buy the world."[7]

Curtis's career took a bad turn in September 1891 when he was arrested on suspicion of murdering a veteran San Francisco police officer. "Curtis, who had been intoxicated and was arrested at the corner of Folsom and Fifth streets, was on his way to the station in the officer's custody," Pete Fanning, a former San Francisco cop, wrote in *Great Crimes Of The West*. "The nippers which the murdered policeman had twisted on his refractory prisoner's wrist were still there to evidence that he was the man who had committed the bloody deed." Curtis blamed an unidentified third man for the killing.[8]

Three trials—each packed with denizens of the theater—did not result in conviction, however. The first ended in a hung jury; the second ended when a juror died; and the third acquitted him. But legal expenses broke him.[9]

Curtis went on to manage several theater companies and even returned to Sam'l of Posen. But when he died in 1920, the *Los Angeles Times* announced, "Old actor once rich dies poor."[10]

How Berkeley Got Religion

The best spot to contemplate Berkeley's spiritual essence is from Holy Hill, a grouping of theological institutes that looks down upon the neighboring university—but in a good way. On Holy Hill—amidst courtyards both modern and Gothic, beneath stained glass windows and live oak trees, and at several scattered sites elsewhere in town—you'll find more than a dozen religious schools and other institutions, Protestant, Catholic and Jewish, nine of them united beneath the umbrella of the Graduate Theological Union.

"Only the chant of the Bible reading class in the chapel can be heard above the buzzing of bees in the grass," Helen Benedict observed in 1980, writing for the *Berkeley Independent* and the *Gazette*.[1]

"The city is not known for training ministers," she added. Nonetheless, Berkeley is one of the leading centers for theological education in the country, thanks to the Pacific School of Religion, the Church Divinity School of the Pacific, the American Baptist Seminary of the West, the Franciscan School of Theology, the Center for Judaic Studies, and others, along with a shared library that has a wonderful little art gallery.

Besides members of the theological union, also on or near the hill, is the LDS (Mormon) Berkeley Institute of Religion, the Institute of Buddhist Studies, and the Tibetan Nyingma Institute.

The schools, which started at various spots around the Bay, gradually made their way to the hill, turning it holy in the 1920s. The Graduate Theological Union formed in 1962 to share resources and staff, and to offer stronger programs than individual schools could do on their own. Over the years, the schools have offered innovative classes, many geared to the community—"mysticism East and West," "the pastor as community strategist." The Pacific School of Religion has a center for urban black studies.

And over the years, everybody has gotten along. The schools represent the more liberal church traditions. "It may not be Utopia," Rebecca Parker, president of the Starr King School for the Ministry, said in 1993, "but it is a foretaste of Utopia."[2]

Churches in Berkeley, often led by Holy Hill graduates, have always gotten involved in community affairs—from the days of Temperance to the troubles in the 1960s.

Holy Hill is emblematic of the town as a whole. Berkeley has always been a highly spiritual place—a place where religion is taken seriously as a force in society. Graduates of its seminaries and people associated with them have helped define the Berkeley ethos.

When Telegraph Avenue and downtown were convulsed with riots over Vietnam and People's Park, and teenage dropouts crowded the town, Reverend Dick York was delegated by the Episcopalians at the Divinity School of the Pacific to help. The result was the Berkeley Free Church, complete with Christian be-ins and free food with health care for all.

When Jane Fonda and Tom Hayden wed, York performed the nuptials.

But no divine has ever been more Berkeley than William Badè, whose liberal scientific take on religion and love of nature made him a central figure from the mid-1900s until his death in 1936. Badè, who grew up a poor Minnesota farm boy and a Moravian by religion, studied ancient languages by candlelight—"Lincoln-like," it was said.[3]

By 1907, he was in Berkeley, where he became professor of Old Testament literature at the Pacific School of Religion. Badè fell in love with the Berkeley Hills, became longtime secretary and president of the Sierra Club, trekked with Muir in the Sierra, edited several of Muir's books, and fought for wildland protection nationwide.

Badè's article "The Old Testament in Light of To-Day," treating the Bible as a historical document that could be interpreted not through exegesis alone but through scientific methods, angered fundamentalists. Many of Badè's colleagues were "astonished, disturbed, alarmed."[4]

Badè led several archeological expeditions to the Holy Land, revealing the site of Tell en-Nasbeh north of Jerusalem. Badè, who pioneered scientific excavation, learned much about Iron Age Palestine. At Tell en-Nasbeh, he opened 672 rooms, 397 bins and cisterns, and dozens of tombs.

He kept friends in Berkeley apprised of his efforts by cabling dispatches to the *Gazette*, describing cisterns and tombs as well as treasures uncountable. "The Egyptian government has been most liberal with us, giving us practically all the pieces we dis-

1900: William Badè at his excavation of Tell en-Nasbeh, also known as the Mizpah ("Watchtower") of Benjamin. Courtesy of Badè Museum, Pacific School of Religion.

1920s: The Pacific School of Religion, which contains the Badè Museum, first brought the "holy" to Holy Hill. Postcard courtesy of Sarah Wikander.

covered in most of the tombs," he reported in 1926.[5] His dispatches were as much about the he hiked past as they were about the owls, insects, frogs, and lizards. The newspaper noted: "Badè has the beginnings of the finest Oriental museum west of Chicago."[6]

Which of his discoveries excited Roaring-Twenties Berkeley most?

Places

Holy Hill is better-tended and quieter than the Cal campus just below. The Badè Museum of Biblical Archeology can be visited at 1798 Scenic Avenue.

That of a statue of Astarte. Rescued from a 3,000-year-old tomb, it proved without doubt that ancient goddesses bobbed their hair.

How Berkeley Developed Its Personality

How Berkeley Became Bohemian

Berkeleyans began hobnobbing quickly. The year the university opened in town, discussion societies started along with the Berkeley Club for Men and the Ebell Society for Ladies. Professors lectured in people's homes. Talks were followed by socializing and singing.

From the very beginning, Berkeley was creating a reputation it has never lost—being a place where artists, philosophers, scientists, theologians, activists, and kibitzers love to make their opinions known. It quickly became a town where artists and writers held sway and has remained so ever since.

In 1881, the psychology club dealt with mind reading. They met at the home of Josiah Royce, who became one of the nation's leading philosophers after he fled the backwater known as Berkeley. "Most of the evening was taken up in experiments, some of which were quite successful," the *Occident* reported.[1]

But in Berkeley, *la vie Bohème* kept its voice down. Berkeley Bohemians were prosperous and hardworking, not living in garrets nor drinking cheap wine. They were to be found less in cafes than at churches—the First Unitarian Church in Berkeley and the Swedenborgian Church in San Francisco's Pacific Heights—or at garden parties, musicals, and private theatricals. Berkeley's Hillside Club and the campus's Harmon Gymnasium were venues for concerts and lectures.

Perhaps Berkeley never developed into a raucous artists' hangout because the artists it could have clustered about—architect Bernard Maybeck and painter William Keith—spent all their time working. In fact, Berkeley's early Bohemians seem downright puritanical. Maybeck stopped drinking and smoking when his wife, Annie—who was the brains behind both his business and household—told him to.

As for Keith: "At one time," his friend Eugen Neuhaus recalled, "he had the habit of allowing himself a drink of Scotch whiskey on the way to the ferry, but when he discovered that this indulgence was taking place at ever earlier periods in the afternoon, it is typical of his character that he at once cut the practice from his daily routine."[2]

Florence and Charles Boynton, Nut Hill's freest spirits, once loved attending Sam Hume's plays at the Greek Theatre—but halted after finding one steeped in immorality. And twenty-one-year-old poet Charles Keeler revealed something of his life philosophy in a petulant letter sent to his girlfriend Louise, later his wife, when he discovered she'd been dancing.

"Of course it was a very mild beginning but was it to end there? To you and from your point of view dancing may be as innocent as counting your beads, but I look at it from a different point of view—as a whole—as a system with infinite shades of gradation from the quiet little family dance at home to the public ballroom and what is not but a little worse, the multitude of saloons and dance halls where men and women waste what little there is of their good-for-nothing lives."[3]

Still, Berkeleyans could hop almost every night from one artistic gathering to another, mixing professors of philosophy and physics with musicians, businessmen, and mountaineers.

"Flaming red poppies, strikingly arranged in huge brass vases" greeted guests to weekly musicals in the early 1900s at Charles Dutton's "quaint studio with its hundred candles burning in their brass sticks."[4] Dutton's motto: "Live music as well as make music." The studio, on Le Roy Avenue north of campus, was shaded by grand oaks.

Frequent guests and performers were Frederick Wolle, a conductor known for his interpretations of Wagner, and pianist Frederick Maurer, "a dreamer and poet by nature," according to *Courier* columnist Madame Pensée.[5]

Oscar Maurer, whose nearby photography studio was designed by Maybeck, also hosted frequent get-togethers with his wife, Margaret Robinson, a founder of the Hillside Club and an early proponent of blending homes into the landscape.

Theatricals, often with elaborate costumes and original music, were a mainstay for these at-home Bohemians. Many brown-shingled homes designed by Maybeck and the other Arts and Crafts architects of the early twentieth century included stages or living rooms designed with performances in mind.

Keeler's Live Oak Guild, founded in 1905 to create "a distinct California drama," opened with Keeler's "Vivian of San Luis Rey," with sets by Maybeck.[6] Architect and poet John Galen Howard also contributed a play to the series.

The preferred venue, however, seems to have been out of doors. The Greek Theatre opened in 1903 and provided inspiration through a series of classically themed pageants. When Keeler built his third home on a hidden hillside in the Claremont district circa 1910, he included a Greek-style amphitheater. Professor Joel

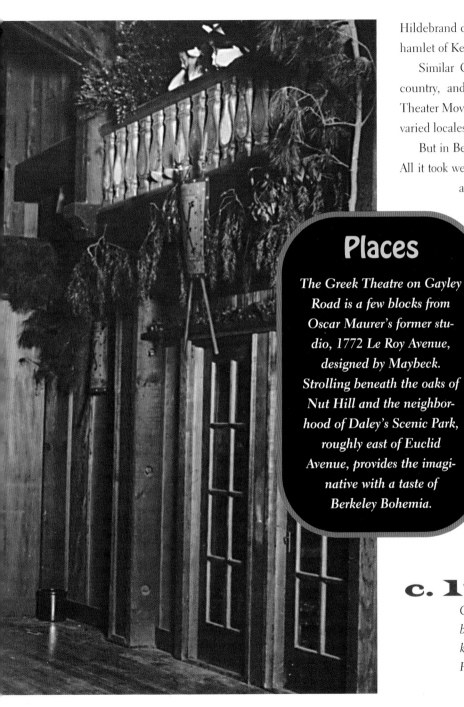

Hildebrand did the same behind his home in the nearby hamlet of Kensington in the 1920s.

Similar Greek-style theaters popped up around the country, and Berkeley helped inspire both the Little Theater Movement and outdoor playhouses, built in such varied locales as Carmel and Jones Beach, New York.

But in Berkeley, an amphitheater wasn't really needed. All it took were a few trees. "Idyll is staged by local author among oaks," the *Berkeley Independent* reported in 1912.[7] More than three hundred guests sat on a hillside to watch R. W. Osborn's "Spirit of the Oaks," performed in a ravine below his home "in the high hills of Berkeley." Mark White, Maybeck's brother-in-law, played a Druid.

Outside of Keith, whose art was nationally esteemed and much copied, few Berkeley Bohemians won national reputations. Maybeck did—but only when he was quite old. But the attitude toward life that developed in Berkeley—that life is best lived amidst art and out of doors—has been widely imbibed.

Places

The Greek Theatre on Gayley Road is a few blocks from Oscar Maurer's former studio, 1772 Le Roy Avenue, designed by Maybeck. Strolling beneath the oaks of Nut Hill and the neighborhood of Daley's Scenic Park, roughly east of Euclid Avenue, provides the imaginative with a taste of Berkeley Bohemia.

c. 1900: *A pageant at the Hillside Club, c. 1900. Bernard Maybeck's rustic building later burned and was replaced in kind. Courtesy of Berkeley Architectural Heritage Association.*

How Berkeley Donned Tunics

Florence Treadwell Boynton

Before deciding that early Berkeley doesn't deserve its reputation for Bohemian living, consider the Boyntons. There was Charles Boynton, in stiff collar and wire rim spectacles—an attorney whose interest in water rights had him arguing before the U.S. Supreme Court. Then there was his wife, Florence Treadwell Boynton, known as "Mina."

Mina grew up in Oakland with the soon-to-be-legendary dancer Isadora Duncan, who was one of the creators of modern dance. Mina, also a dancer, almost married Isadora's brother, which would have taken her to Europe, where much of Duncan's career was spent. But her parents said no. Instead, Mina became a legend of her own.

In Alameda, where she and Charles first settled, she went around the house without shoes. "Are you going to let your sons see your bare feet?" her father demanded. A believer in healthful outdoor living, Mina spent nights on her sleeping porch, shocking neighbors. Even worse, she gave birth to her son Ben Fay in an outdoor arbor. The papers wrote it up. Mina's fame was ensured.

By 1914 Charles and Mina, and their growing family—eight children, eventually—were living above the campus in the Temple of the Wings, a swooping colonnade of Corinthian columns with absolutely no exterior walls. The Boyntons hoisted canvas when necessary.

The Boyntons cooked and entertained outside. The Temple's flooring was made of hollow tiles with radiant hot air heating to keep feet warm while dancing. It also kept the family warm at night. They slept on mats that rolled up during the day.

"He was a very admirable man," Charles Quitzow said of his father-in-law, Charles Boynton. "He didn't understand art at all, but his wife loved it so he put up with it."

"She kept him . . . well, entertained isn't the word. But she just continually amazed him," added Sulgwynn Boynton Quitzow, Quitzow's wife, in a 1973 oral history, "Dance at the Temple of the Wings: The Boynton-Quitzow Family in Berkeley."[1]

Why did the Boyntons have so many children? "Children are the thoughts of God," Mina explained.

Mina, who lobbied for open-air schools, fed the family largely on fruit, raisins, nuts, cheese, and butter; they would eat meat at restaurants, however. And, as their friend Jacomena Maybeck recalled, "The eight children took nuts and raisins as their lunches at school. But they traded them for bologna sandwiches."[2]

Mina may remain a footnote in the

c. 1915: *Florence Treadwell Boynton ("Mina") and brood in the curtain-walled Temple of the Wings. Courtesy of Berkeley Architectural Heritage Association.*

Places

A portion of the Temple, a private residence, can be spotted from the street at 2800 Buena Vista Way. Or stand at 2420 Ridge Road on Holy Hill and scan the hills with binoculars. Boynton Avenue is named for the family.

history of vegetarianism, but her insistence on living without walls certainly contributed to Berkeley's influential tradition of coexisting with nature.

Everyone recognized the Boynton children—they wore loose-fitting tunics of their mother's design. "She thought children needed more fresh air and fewer clothes and more freedom in movement," Sulgwynn said. "She felt that all the long underwear, keeping the air away from the body, was wrong."

During the day, the Temple served as a dance pavilion, with Mina teaching classes for little pay. At night they often opened the Temple to "at-homes," serving cheese biscuits and hosting poetry readings, concerts, and dancing—before the rising moon whenever possible.

It wasn't always easy being a Boynton, even in Berkeley. "People would say, 'Oh, you're one of the crazy Boyntons from that hill,'" said Oeloel Quitzow Brown, Charles and Sulgwynn's daughter. "Kids get upset by things like that."

"The family came to be looked upon as queers," Charles Quitzow admitted in 1972, when hippies were taking over the town. "They ate differently, they dressed differently, they had different ideas. I don't hear so much of that anymore. The family got away with it! It looks like they're getting outdone now!"

c. 1915: *Dancers circle the maypole at the Temple of the Wings. Courtesy of Berkeley Architectural Heritage Association.*

How Berkeley Revealed Nature's Spirit

William Keith

By the time he hit forty years old, William Keith was selling his paintings to the titans of the day—Leland Stanford, A. K. P. Harmon, Mark Hopkins. Collis P. Huntington, one of the "Big Four," as were Stanford, Crocker, and Hopkins, advised friends, "Buy Keiths."[1]

Eugen Neuhaus, who founded the university's art department, was a friend, though he found friendship challenging at times. "I was able to obtain a vacant studio opposite his because nobody wanted to be opposite Keith since he was so offensively prosperous," Neuhaus wrote. "It was painful to see clients traipsing into his studio and passing everyone else by."[2]

It astonished his friend Leon Richardson that Keith could paint so assiduously—he turned out hundreds of paintings a year—while entertaining a steady stream of guests in his San Francisco studio.

These included his close friend, John Muir (both Scots, they called each other Johnnie and Willie, and tramped the Sierra together), Charles Keeler, writers Edward Robinson Taylor and Ina Coolbrith, designer Bruce Porter, historian Theodore Hittell, and strangers.

The unflappable Keith didn't even mind criticism—at least if it came from Muir. Keeler recalled visiting the studio with Muir to find "Keith expounding on the merits of his pictures to an admiring crowd." Johnnie found little to admire, however, in one painting. "He said he had been in the Yosemite at all times and had never seen it look anything like that picture."[3]

Muir preferred Keith's earlier realistic paintings to his later mystical ones. "The painted rocks are so truly rocky, you would expect to hear them clank and ring to the blows of a hammer," Muir wrote of Keith's early *The Headwaters of the Merced.*[4]

But it was Keith's later more-spiritual paintings that best represented the man's attitude toward life—an attitude that is altogether Berkeley in its appreciation for the essence that hides behind appearance. Keith may have been a mystic—but he was a realist too, working with his friend John Muir to preserve the out of doors that he loved.

Visitors to Keith's studio were often entertained by more than paint. Student Emily P. B. Hay remembered how Keith would sing while painting. "Thrusting his hands through his leonine locks, he would sound a few disconnected notes," she wrote, "follow them with brief and prolonged pauses, then, glancing over his shoulder to enjoy the tension of our nerves, suddenly plunge into phenomena of strange harmonies and agonizing discords surely illustrative of some cataclysm in nature."[5]

But outside his studio and his home, Keith rarely socialized. "He is an excellent storyteller and mimic," Keeler wrote, "has a good tenor voice, and, in fact, is well-equipped for a boon companion on a frolic; but the habitual seriousness of his nature and his absorption in his work prevent him, except occasionally in his own home, among a few chosen friends, from exercising these talents."[6]

Keith, whose lifes pan (1838–1911) almost exactly matched Muir's, lived across from campus. He liked nothing better than walking through the Berkeley hills with his dogs, Hegel and Jumbo. "Sometimes in the evening, in a playful mood," Neuhaus reported, "he would take one of them by the forelegs and dance around the room with him."

A conservationist, Keith worked with Muir to preserve Yosemite. He was friends with Berkeley's early conservationists, including Joseph Le Conte, Little Joe Le Conte, and Bill Colby.

Keith, who first met Muir in 1872 in Yosemite, trekked with him often in the Sierra, Alaska, and British Columbia. He spent a few weeks most summers with Muir in the mountains, and when Muir fought to save the Hetch Hetchy Valley, Keith joined in the fight, speaking out in public and writing letters to the press.

Keith's wife, an attorney, was a leader of the women's rights movement and bragged that her husband was a "New Man" who developed "his own self-respect by according respect to all women, the bad as well as the good."[7]

Keith, like Muir (who believed he had powers of telepathy), was a mystic, "saturating himself in 'suggestion,' 'thought transference,' 'phantoms of the living and the dead,' " Emily Hay wrote. He even used mystic means when he painted.

Keith painted next to "a set of Japanese temple gongs, whose bulging and spacious forms he would set in vibration with a large wooden clapper, with resultant sonorous deep sounds," Neuhaus wrote. "The rich, mellow chords thus produced would inspire him to seek an equivalent in terms of color and tones."

1880s: *William Keith.*
Courtesy of the Bancroft Library of the University of California, Berkeley.

Places

The Oakland Museum and the de Young Museum in San Francisco are rife with Keith's work. But by far the best collection is at the Hearst Art Gallery at St. Mary's College in Moraga.

Keith was influenced by the Reverend Joseph Worcester, whose Swedenborgian Church in Presidio Heights was a refuge for many of the Bay Area's Arts and Crafts designers. "Silently— for an hour, perhaps, Mr. Worcester sits lost in contemplation of a landscape forming on the Master's easel," Hay wrote of a typical visit to Keith's studio.

"Hardly a day goes by," she wrote of Keith, "that he does not ascend the height of Russian Hill to lunch with his clerical companion on nuts and cocoa and subsequently to ascend other heights whose crests are eternally unattainable."

1870s: Glacial Meadow and Lake, High Sierra Tuolumne Meadows *by Keith from the 1870s to early 1880s. Courtesy the Hearst Art Gallery, Saint Mary's College of California. Gift of Dr. William S. Porter.*

How Berkeley Promoted the Good Life

Charles Keeler

Few men set their goals so early or stuck to them so consistently as Charles Keeler, who decided as a boy to become a naturalist and poet, and spent the rest of his life pursuing both goals—despite notable failures.

Although he wrote one book, *The Simple Home*, which helped define the Berkeley look and remains a classic, Keeler's other poetical productions—ballads, pageants, children's verse ("Elfin Songs of Sunland"), novels, nature books, journalism, and radio plays—are forgotten. And, though his homes in Berkeley were showpieces of his harmonious living-with-nature lifestyle, Keeler lived much of his life hand to mouth.

Still, no one came closer than Keeler to formulating a Theory of Berkeley or to living it: Life is best when lived out of doors. Your home should belong to nature. Fine art should be inhaled like air. Figure out what is best for your community and make it happen. Study nature but don't ignore spirit. An evening is best spent with friends listening to music or attending the theater, or making your own music and theater.

Bernard Maybeck designed a brown-shingled home for Keeler in 1895, helping set the rustic yet playful-and-sophisticated look of the Berkeley Hills for decades to come. Keeler put Maybeck's Arts and Crafts aesthetic into words and turned it into a crusade.

Keeler made his mark at Cal by establishing the Evolution Club to promote Darwin's theory, which was so controversial it split friendships. For Keeler, though, evolution led to love. After spotting the club's leader, with his long hair and intense brown eyes, coed Louise Mapes Bunnell developed a sudden interest in Darwin. They married a few years later and collaborated—Louise as designer—on some of the best Arts and Crafts publications produced in the Bay Area.

By 1892 Keeler was working at the California Academy of Science and exploring the fauna of the Farallones Islands. His first book came out the next year, *The Evolution of Colors of North American Land*

1905:

Keeler in Greek robes, modeling for his wife Louise, who was illustrating his "Triumph of Light." Courtesy of the Berkeley Architectural Heritage Association.

Birds. In 1899, he accompanied Muir, naturalist John Burroughs, and other scientists on the Harriman expedition to Alaska, forming friendships that would last. He hiked with Muir in the Sierra and helped form the Sierra Club.

In Berkeley, when the women who founded the Hillside Club to advocate naturalistic planning in the Hills needed men in their organization to give it political clout (this was before women had the vote), Keeler became president and molded it into an activist organization and political force. The club fought for winding streets that followed the contours of the land, for tree preservation, and for architecture that blended with the landscape. The club's principles were based on Maybeck's architecture and Keeler's theories. Keeler's ambitions, as ever, were huge. He saw the club becoming a statewide movement. It never did, but its principles and successes still inspire anyone who visits the Berkeley Hills.

Like most of Berkeley's artists and writers, Keeler was stylistically conservative. "The great problem with regard to beauty as I see it today," he wrote a friend in 1929, "is that the so-called 'new art,' modernistic art, encourages and glorifies ugliness in the name of art . . . They are in fact psychopathic schizophrenics in whom the normal standards of beauty in nature have been swept away and their grotesque fantasies have supplanted them."[1]

Places

Keeler Avenue, a typically charming residential street high in the Berkeley Hills, meets the rustic Keeler Path at Remillard Park.

After Louise died in 1907—she had been ill and weakened after spending weeks helping San Francisco earthquake refugees in Berkeley—Keeler found himself raising three children by himself. (He finally remarried in 1921, after staving off his suitor for years, pleading poverty.)

His mother watched the children while Keeler took his show on the road, attracting 250 Europeans to a reading at Tokyo's Imperial Hotel in 1911, followed by successes in Hong Kong and Manila. He performed in Paris and London, met every literary figure he cared to, and settled in New York.

But Keeler had little luck outside Berkeley. He spent his days hustling after his one big break and his nights writing in a series of increasingly shabby rooms. "My days are so very full that I go from one appointment to the next with the regularity of a machine," he wrote home. "It is all in the line of making my work known, but so far without decisive result."[2]

Keeler had successes. His poem "The Enchanted Forest," which he wrote in three nights between midnight and 2 a.m., attracted a full audience to the Waldorf-Astoria. His daughter, "poor little Eloise," fainted from the excitement. Still, without his mother's checks, he would have been unable to pay the rent, and by 1917, Keeler "really feared I might find myself here with no money to pay for my room or to buy food."

Home by the start of World War I, Keeler was back to form, involving himself with the Rotary and Bohemian clubs, attending salons, and writing incessantly. For seven years Keeler had the unusual experience, for a poet, of managing the Chamber of Commerce. It was a job he handled well, boosting dues while quadrupling membership and tackling such divisive issues as the future of Berkeley waterfront, which he hoped to preserve largely as open space. His stance cost him the job.

Keeler had already embarked on a project he hoped would gain him worldwide acclaim, or at least a dependable salary—the Cosmic Society. "If civilization is to survive, a new religious consciousness must help to unite the world," he wrote. His religion was based on "the common religious bond in which all religions share," "the trinity of love, truth and beauty."[3]

Keeler based the society's organization on that of the Chamber and the Rotary Club, and expected to serve as its paid director. He tried to start branches in Los Angeles and Washington, D.C., and insisted, "If Cosmic Religion societies are organized, they will be required to receive their charters from the Berkeley headquarters."

The society often met before the fireplace at Charles and Sulgwynn Quitzow's Passmore studio or at Mary McHenry Keith's hillside home. Evenings featured piano, violin, or vocal recitals. Members—about fifty—would also talk about their lives and would patronize each others' businesses.

Keeler's plans for a Cosmic Temple were characteristically ambitious. "Within such a temple would be the magic of modern lighting producing strangely beautiful effects falling upon moving water, stained glass designs, mural paintings symbolic of Cosmic Religion, sculpture and carvings," Keeler wrote. "There would be organ music, chamber music, a symphony orchestra and choir, dramatic pageants and allegories rendered."[4]

The temple, in other words, would not have been brown shingled.

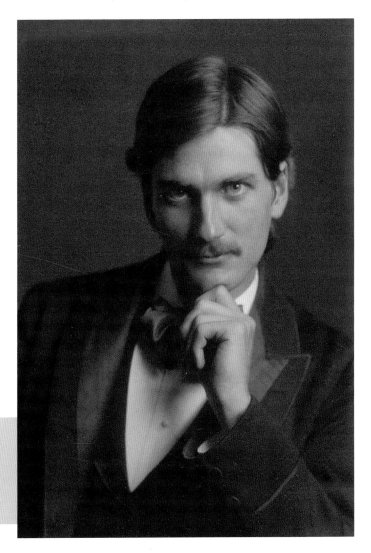

c. 1894: *Charles Keeler. Courtesy of the Bancroft Library of the University of California, Berkeley.*

How Berkeley Developed Its Look

Bernard Maybeck

"The exterior of a house should always be conceived so that it will harmonize with its surroundings," Charles Keeler wrote in *The Simple Home*, a 1905 exhortation based largely on the work of his friend, architect Bernard Maybeck. "The safest means of effecting this is by leaving the natural material to the tender care of the elements."

"Ornament should grow out of the construction, and should always be an individual expression adapted to the particular space it is to fill. Thus all machine-turned moldings, sawed-out brackets, or other mechanical devices for ornament, may well be rigorously excluded."

All of this, of course, was as much about moral improvement as interior decor. "A large nature may rise above his environment and live in a dream world of his own fashioning," Keeler wrote, "but most of us are mollusks after all, and are shaped and sized by the walls which we build about us."

Arts and Crafts design seized control of towns across America toward the end of the nineteenth century—but nowhere so idiosyncratically as it did in the Bay Area. Besides Maybeck, such architects as A. Page Brown, Willis Polk, Ernest Coxhead, A. C. Schweinfurth, and Julia Morgan turned out quirky churches, public buildings, and especially houses, defining what came to be called "The First Bay Tradition."

The Craftsman-look faded, but its mark on Berkeley remains sure. Shingled or wood-sided houses fit so well among the live oaks that dot the hills. And many post–World War II architects added their own take on the Bay Area

Bernard Maybeck *in characteristic costume at his concrete sack house in the Berkeley Hills. Courtesy of the Berkeley Architectural Heritage Association.*

home, marrying high-end modernism—glass walls, modular designs, open plans—with redwood warmth. Many of these "Second Bay Tradition" architects were explicitly influenced by Maybeck and Morgan's "First Bay Tradition" work.

The influence of the First Bay Tradition, its attitudes as much as its look, spread beyond the Bay Area. It can be seen in Southern California in the work of Harwell Harris and A. Quincy Jones, among others. It can even be detected in open-plan, wood-sided ski lodges and beach houses throughout the country and in many homes in which rusticity of materials blends with a modern outlook toward planning and space.

Maybeck had an especially strong impact in Berkeley because

of his designs for so many houses north of campus (an area he helped develop), because of his role in planning the campus and because of his personality, which comes across in his buildings.

There's a wit about a Maybeck building, a joy that is hard to miss. Though trained at the École des Beaux-Arts in Paris, he was always a bit of an outsider architect—too inventive to be constrained by style. Maybeck designed superbly in the high-art classical traditions. But his houses in Berkeley tended to be odd combinations of the rustic, fantastical, storybook, and industrial. After the Berkeley fire of 1923, he pioneered such fire-resistant materials as sacks soaked in concrete and laid over a scaffolding of metal.

1910: *The interior of Maybeck's First Church of Christ, Scientist, at 2619 Dwight Way, blends Gothic with touches of modern industrial. Courtesy of the Bancroft Library of the University of California, Berkeley.*

1899: *Maybeck's fantastical Hearst Hall, built in 1899 at the university, thanks to Phoebe Hearst, gives a taste of his genius. It was lost to fire in 1922. Postcard courtesy of Sarah Wikander.*

Maybeck's famous Sack House served as an example of a low-cost, fire-resistant house that could be easily replicated. "Anybody can do it himself," Maybeck told writer Winthrop Sargeant. "All you need is old sacks, a few beams and that porous cement."[1]

To show off the material, Maybeck tore some out of the walls. "Maybeck has shown his floating cement to so many visitors that he is in danger of pulling his whole house to pieces for demonstration," Sargeant wrote.

Ben, as he was called, with his "Pooh bear figure, the beard, the sparkling eyes," cut quite a figure in town, his daughter-in-law Jacomena Maybeck wrote. When kids spotted Maybeck in his red beret, being driven home by his

Places

Many Maybeck homes can be spotted on Nut Hill, including the Lawson house on 1515 La Loma Avenue and the Sack House at 2711 Buena Vista. Julia Morgan's St. John's Presbyterian Church—today the Julia Morgan Center—is at 2640 College Avenue. A. C. Schweinfurth's First Unitarian Church at 2401 Bancroft Avenue on the university campus—now a dance studio—was another trendsetting masterpiece.

daughter, Kerna, in a silver-and-black Packard, they'd wave and yell, "Hi, Santa Claus."[2]

His wife, Annie, "little and pretty and shy," handled the family business—including the real estate transactions that kept them prosperous. "She sold land, borrowed on it, and gave it away," Jacomena wrote. "She sold lots only to 'nice young people who did not smoke or drink or get divorced.' "

Annie also kept Ben on the straight and narrow. "She made him stop smoking and drinking wine, took over all his finances, and was fierce as a tiger in his behalf."

1900: *A. C. Schweinfurth's First Unitarian Church, with posts still bearing their tree bark and an abstract design, exemplifies the Bay Tradition in architecture. Postcard courtesy of Sarah Wikander.*

Sargeant, who visited when Maybeck was eighty-five, found a man who "talks gravely and unsmirkingly about things like God and beauty." Maybeck, long retired, was outside his small concrete house developing a plan to rebuild San Francisco with elegant boulevards.

"One of his favorite relaxations," Sargeant reported, "is crooning whole scenes from obscure French operas, singing coloratura soprano and bass parts with equal intrepidity and expert French diction."

How Berkeley's University Cultivated a Beautiful Campus

The hills were stupendous, its glades serene, Strawberry Creek a torrent, but the ensemble of Victorian buildings placed upon the early university campus struck many as an insult to nature.

"The grounds of the university, selected by the founders for their peculiarly attractive qualities, have been treated with no more consideration than if they were so many acres of an alkali patch in the San Joaquin Valley," wrote William Carey Jones, founder of the law school.[1]

It was the mid-1890s, and Stanford had just gotten its Inner Quad and Memorial Church, a gorgeous medieval cloister of sandstone. University Regent Jacob Reinstein decided that Berkeley needed a new campus. And architect Bernard Maybeck "not only saw the things that are and regretted the things that might have been, but sketched in his mind the things that might still be," Jones wrote.

Maybeck proposed not that he be given the job of designing the campus, but that the university seek the best plan possible by sponsoring an international competition of a scope never before seen. That's when Phoebe Apperson said, "Let me help in that."[2] Soon The Phoebe Apperson Hearst architectural plan for the University of California was underway, with Reinstein and Maybeck meeting architects on the East Coast and in Europe, seeking applicants with a prospectus in German, French, and English.

The competition won worldwide fame for the university. "The best work that can be found in the world is wanted," Harper's Weekly reported. About Maybeck, Harper's said: "His dream was one of pure beauty; there was no consideration of cost in it, any more than in the mind of Aladdin when he ordered his attendant genii to create him a palace."[3]

The first judging took place in Antwerp, the second in 1898 in San Francisco. Judges enjoyed a banquet at the Bohemian Grove and a reception with Mayor James D. Phelan under the dome at San Francisco's new city hall. Jurors dined with Phoebe Hearst at her Hacienda in Pleasanton and climbed Mount Tam.

1914: *John Galen Howard's cover for his 1914 campus plan shows the Beaux-Arts classical ideal. Courtesy of the Bancroft Library of the University of California, Berkeley.*

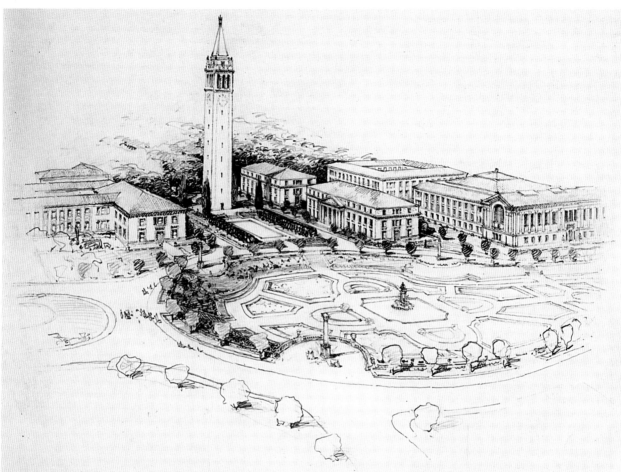

SATHER TOWER   NORTH HALL   UNIVERSITY LIBRARY

PHOEBE APPERSON HEARST
PLAN
UNIVERSITY of CALIFORNIA

JOHN GALEN HOWARD
ARCHITECT.

1909: *Workers constructing Sather Gate in 1909. Courtesy of the Bancroft Library of the University of California, Berkeley.*

c. 1912: *Phoebe Apperson Hearst deserved her regal air. Courtesy of the Berkeley Historical Society, 490.190 3414.*

The University Library Building, Berkeley, Cal.

10528.

c. 1910: *Doe Library, which began construction in 1907, is one of John Galen Howard's jewels, with a spectacular reading room. Postcard courtesy of Sarah Wikander.*

The winner was the Émile Bénard plan, "a total ensemble fit for the Olympian gods," according to the *San Francisco Bulletin.*[4] But relations between Bénard and the regents soured, and it fell to John Galen Howard, whose plan had been a runner-up, to carry out the scheme. The results became more Howard than Bénard, and Howard was soon as Bay Area an architect as you could find. Besides overseeing the building of the campus, he founded the Department of Architecture.

How Berkeley Founded National Parks

his is a grandeur incomparable!" Joseph Le Conte announced, gesturing over Yosemite Valley. "The most wonderful sight in nature!"[1] It was 1870, the University of California geologist's first trip to the valley. His companions included John Muir, who'd first visited the valley only two years before. Now Muir did whatever it took to stay there—breaking horses, running a ferry, working at a nearby hotel, and even shearing sheep, an animal he despised because of its depredations on the land.

The Muir-Berkeley connection was forged on this trip, and it would be crucial for the development of parks in America. Over the next four decades, Muir, who lived in Martinez, twenty-five miles from Berkeley, would create the impetus for Yosemite National Park as we know it today, as well as the National Park System and the Sierra Club. Many of the people who worked with him were from Berkeley, and it was in Berkeley that the popular Sierra Club mountain excursions were pioneered.

Muir, whom Charles Keeler recalls as "a very pleasant rugged Scotchman with long curly hair and a merry twinkle in his eye," could have become a Thomas Edison.[2] As a boy in Wisconsin, he invented an "early-riser" machine that got slugabeds up and at 'em by literally tipping them out of bed. As a young man, Muir helped broom and carriage makers improve their manufacturing, but all he cared about was exploring nature in as intimate a manner as possible—tramping a *Thousand Mile Walk to the Gulf*, as he described in his first book, or getting messy in a Sierra creek:

> "After plashing and laving in the spangling crystal I swam across to examine a section of the bank and found charred bark ten feet below lake and flood deposits," he wrote in 1874 to Jeanne Carr, his mentor.

1890s: *Glacier Point in Yosemite. Photo by Joseph N. Le Conte. Courtesy of the Colby Memorial Library, Sierra Club, historical archives.*

In a vertical position on the bank I discovered two small frogs of a new species each snugly nestled in a dainty nitch from whence they could look out over the water. They are not water frogs however. I swam over with them in my hand holding them aloft and when I ducked them they made a great nervous ado. I have them in my room hoping they may sing like crickets or tree frogs for me in the night."[3]

Muir was also a superb educator and politician, leading anyone through the Sierra that he could convince to visit. "It will cost you nothing save the time," Muir wrote Ralph Waldo Emerson about a proposed trip, "and very little of that for you will be mostly in eternity."[4]

President Theodore Roosevelt was so entranced by his 1903 tour that he shooed off his handlers. He and Muir spent three days in the wilderness. The trip resulted in Roosevelt saving one of Muir's favorite spots, the Hetch Hetchy Valley.

Marion Randall Parsons, Little Joe Le Conte, William Badè, developer Duncan McDuffie, and Bill Colby were other Berkeley figures who were prominent leaders of the Sierra Club in its first decades. The club was formed in 1889.

Starting in 1901, Colby began leading caravans with two hundred or more members on month-long excursions to Yosemite, complete with ninety mules, copious amounts of bacon and ham, a French chef and a Chinese cook, fifty packers, and portable stoves of Colby's invention. "I've forgotten how much sugar we took along, but it was a tremendous amount," Colby recalled. "Let's see. It would be a ton and a half."[5]

1880s: *John Muir contemplates the Sierra. Courtesy of the Sierra Club Library.*

The trips were intended to build support for saving the wilderness, and they worked. "As it turned out," Muir said, "when we had a big battle over something it was the people who went on these outings who did the fighting."[6]

The Sierra Club still leads wilderness trips, of course—but not on so industrial a scale.

In later years, other Berkeleyans continued to fight for the Sierra and other conservationist causes. The first director of the National Park Service, Stephen T. Mather, graduated from Cal in 1887, joined the Sierra Club, and became trekking buddies with Muir, Colby, and Joseph Le Conte. And David Brower, Berkeley born and bred, was the Sierra Club's longtime executive director starting in 1952 and founder of the more radical Friends of the Earth.

Muir won no greater convert than Joseph Le Conte, who had helped the Confederate states as a chemist and moved to California with misgivings. He was one of Cal's most popular professors, with "his great head of snowy hair shining like a halo about him." He would lecture using "a voice of wonderful flexibility and it followed with perfect naturalness every phrase of his theme."[7]

A religious man, Le Conte only gradually accepted evolution—then won fame for combining it with religion. "Without immortality," Le Conte argued, "this whole purpose is balked—the whole process of cosmic evolution is futile."[8]

Le Conte traveled to the Sierra at least annually. He'd quote poetry while hiking and always carried a sketchbook, capturing both the awesome peaks and the foibles of his fellow campers.

At age seventy-seven Le Conte rode on horseback to the summit of Kearsage Pass. That night in camp he felt pain on the left side of his chest—his angina. Still, he enjoyed a hearty dinner. The next morning, after a doctor's visit, the pain returned. Then, according to his friend, Professor Frank Soulé, Le Conte's daughter advised him not to lie on his left side. "It does not matter, daughter," Le Conte said, and died.[9]

1900: *A picnic in Yosemite, with Little Joe Le Conte, left, his wife, and Professor Joseph Le Conte, right. Courtesy of the Colby Memorial Library, Sierra Club, historical archives.*

Places

The David Brower Center is located across from the campus on Oxford Street. The John Muir National Historic Site preserves his house and surroundings in Martinez; and Berkeley has its Muir Way and Muir Path. Le Conte Hall and Le Conte Avenue are named after brothers John and Joseph.

By the 1910s, Muir was a legendary figure nationwide, with schools named after him (there's an elementary school in Madison, Wisconsin, among many others), Muir's Peak in Northern California, Muir Glacier in Alaska, Muir Country Park in his native Scotland, Muir Woods National Monument in Marin County, California—and, finally, the John Muir Trail (Little Joe helped choose the route) in the Sierra Nevada mountain range of California. Muir's books were extremely popular, though he hated writing them and grew irritable while so occupied. His wife, Louise, avoided playing the piano when Johnnie was writing, and his daughters walked on tiptoe. Muir lost his final fight in 1913 when Congress passed the Raker Act, authorizing the flooding of his beloved Hetch Hetchy to provide water for San Francisco. "It nearly killed him," Colby said. Muir died the next year.[10]

1903: *Campers at a Sierra Club High trip celebrate July 4 dinner at the Kern River in 1903. Photo by Joseph N. Le Conte. Courtesy of the Colby Memorial Library, Sierra Club, historical archives.*

How Berkeley Became Asian

Berkeley may have been a multicultural city from the start—but it didn't come naturally.

If Berkeley early on proved itself to be as racist a town as most in the country, it also managed to get past its racism—at times, and in ways that suggest the liberal town it would later become. Throughout its history, Berkeley has attracted minority residents—and some people in town often put out the welcome mat. Ultimately, however, the success of Berkeley's minorities depended not on others but on their own talent and perseverance.

In 1878, *Berkeley Advocate* publisher H. N. Marquand called Chinese emigrants "the state's greatest curse." Chinese were working in West Berkeley's soap works, mills, and breweries, and a lot of people didn't like it.[1]

One of these was Dennis Kearney, a San Francisco rabble-rouser whose influence was at its height in the late '70s and early '80s, as was anti-Chinese sentiment. Congress halted immigration with the Chinese Exclusion Act in 1882.

Kearney's Workingmen's Party, which denounced capitalists and Chinese in the same breath, took hold in West Berkeley, with rallies at Willow Grove Park ("a good band has been engaged," the party promised) and sandlot meetings.[2] At one such meeting, Kearney urged his followers to drop bullets for ballots, at least temporarily. Elect a governor, he cried out, elect a mayor, and ensure that twenty thousand like-minded men are armed "before attempting to prevent the landing of Chinamen or the seizure of grain ships to send the Chinaman back to his own country."[3]

For decades, to be an ethnic minority in Berkeley was to be Asian, Finnish, Jewish, Italian, or otherwise eastern or southern European. There were few blacks, Hispanics, or Native Americans.

But Chinese and Japanese were moving to town, setting up small shops, peddling fruit, building communities, and attending the university. Along with all-Caucasian fraternities and sororities, there were Japanese, Chinese, and Filipino student residential clubhouses from early on. Later, in 1930, International House, the first coeducational, interracial

1925: *The university's Chinese Student Club of 1925. Courtesy of the Bancroft Library of the University of California, Berkeley.*

college residence in the western United States, would open just off campus.

Many Asians did well. By 1905, the Japan Brewing Co. in West Berkeley was brewing ninety thousand gallons of "rice nectar"a year and selling it in Hawaii, the Philippines, and Japan. "The Mikado and his court prefer the Berkeley brand to the home stuff," the firm's manager, Mr. Seojima, said. It was the only sake brewery in the states.[4]

Even laundrymen could prosper. Kurasaburo Fujii, who came to America in 1903, became a laundryman in Berkeley in 1910 and organized the larger University Laundry four years later with several other Japanese families. The laundry, located at Shattuck and Blake, had a workspace downstairs, with padded brick irons and drum washers powered by belts and pulleys, and living areas upstairs for owners and their families, complete with communal dining and bathing facilities.[5]

Up at 4:30 a.m. to fire up the boilers, Fujii would eat breakfast with family and crew at 6 o'clock and then work till dusk. After a communal dinner, he'd be back at work till 10 p.m.

But life wasn't all work, his son John Naoki Fujii recalled. The Berkeley United Methodist Church provided a social center. And its pastor, Reverend Nobunda Oda, helped bring to the states daughters whom Kurasaburo and his wife Kikuyu had sent back to Japan before they realized Berkeley would be their permanent home.

On weekends, communal dinners above the laundry would evolve into parties. And relaxing together while soaking in the communal tub could prove amusing as well, Naoki wrote. "This caused difficulties at times between husbands and wives."

By the mid-1920s, when Berkeley had more than five hundred Japanese residents, several of the laundry's owners bought homes. The Fujiis found an attractive, two-story, five-bedroom home on Harper Street. It soon had a garden and chicken coop. They had a piano and taught the children to play; it was a very "American" thing to do.

But racism was never far away, especially in the early years. There was nothing hidden about housing segregation. Asians and blacks had to live in the city's southwestern flatlands, west of Grove Street (today, Martin Luther King Jr. Way) and south of Dwight. Only a handful managed to break this geographic barrier.

In 1903, Berkeley schools provided separate classrooms for Japanese and Chinese children, responding to complaints that teachers were wasting valuable teaching time working with students who couldn't speak English. As reported in the *Gazette*, the Asian children "will not be connected in any way with the other school children of the city . . . The school will be for a half day only, as it is thought that will be all the time that will necessarily be required for the instruction of the Asiatics."[6]

And H. S. Howard's *Berkeley Courier* kept up a drumbeat of hatred. Howard reported with glee whenever neighbors protested against a new steam laundry. "The rumored advent of another Chinese laundry into that section of town aroused the residents of Dwight Way," he wrote in 1905, "for they declared that they had more Chinese there than they wanted already."[7]

But it's clear that not everyone in Berkeley shared Howard's hatred for their Asian neighbors. Howard almost expired after watching "a beautiful, fair-haired little American girl of four summers" playing with a Japanese boy in the "fashionable residence section" across from campus. "So they will grow up together, and perhaps marry in the course of years, breaking the hearts of the American parents, who reproach God for sending this great disgrace upon them. . . Unconscious of the awful danger to the future generation," he noted, "people look placidly on and say, 'How cute.' "[8]

How Berkeley Created a Great University

Naysayers had predicted that the University of California would never become a great school. How could it, being state run? For a time it appeared they were right. In the early 1870s, just as the university was moving to Berkeley, farmers and mechanics across the state led by the Granger Movement were hounding legislators to create a university that taught only practical subjects. As a land grant college, that was what Cal should be all about, they argued. Who needs philosophy, music, or the humanities?

The battle grew nasty. Daniel Coit Gilman, the first president after the university moved to Berkeley, quit in 1875 and moved back East to serve as president of Johns Hopkins in part because of the unrelenting pressure.

When Cal students wanted to put someone down for being a hick, they called him a "granger-looking man."[1] The Grangers wanted to replace the independent Board of Regents with an elected body so political pressure could more easily be applied. They lost. But for years the university remained a gangly adolescent of a school.

Josiah Royce, who graduated in 1875, caught the eye of Gilman, who paid for the brilliant young philosopher to pursue advanced study in Germany. Later, Royce took a position in the English department—but fretted all the while. Berkeley was just too provincial. He hopped to Harvard, filling in for William James.

Still, good men settled into Cal—George Holmes Howison in philosophy, Eugene Hilgard in agricultural science. Cal also benefited from extraordinary philanthropy. It was given a functioning medical school in 1873 and funds from James Lick for an observatory at Mount Hamilton east of San Jose in the mid-1870s.

By 1892, by several objective criteria, Cal was well on its way to greatness. Millicent Shinn, Cal's first woman PhD, back in the days when such an accomplishment was rare, reported in her magazine, *Overland Monthly*, that Cal ranked sixth among American universities in annual income, after Harvard, Columbia, Yale, Michigan, and Cornell. Cal came in seventh in number of students—1,079—and fifth in number of teachers—194.[2]

But it was Benjamin Ide Wheeler—strong willed, sure of himself, a lover of all things German except militarism—who gets most of the credit for turning the university into a major institution. After years of weak presidents, Wheeler insisted upon control over faculty and staff when he took the job in 1899. After years of presidents whose tenures averaged three years, Wheeler served twenty.

In his first report to the Regents, Wheeler announced what was needed—a new library, buildings for student activities and art, schools of forestry and architecture, and more foreign-language instructors. When he left, most had been obtained.

"He found here a provincial college," said another great president, Robert Gordon Sproul, "and he left a great university, known and respected wherever scholars gather."[3]

A sociable man, Wheeler was friends with presidents, railroad barons, and financiers—and the German Kaiser, an association that cost him dearly during the First World War. It may even have cost him his job.

But it was Wheeler's relations with students, who called him "Big Ben," that most characterized his reign. He greeted them by name, often while riding across campus on his horse.

Wheeler never missed a rally nor a game—even though he despised football. He encouraged students to govern themselves and to punish malefactors on their own.

He also started a popular tradition, "Senior Singing," an event "commingled of college songs and yells along with earnest discussion of important problems in student life."[4]

Above all else, Wheeler tried to forge students into self-directed men and women of action. "Think about the things you want to think about," he told them. "Thinking is a scarce article, especially self-guided thinking. Most people do not think at all, or, at the most, barely in dabs and flashes, here and there; what people commonly call their thinking is a mass of dreamy, watery thought-images imposed upon them on hearing or reading the words of others. This means drifting with the current, but real thinking feels the tiller and the keel. It goes where it is told to go."[5]

1910s: *Benjamin Ide Wheeler often rode across campus. Courtesy of the Berkeley Historical Society, 145 GG.*

1930s: *Sather Gate marked the boundary of campus until expansion pushed southwards in the early 1940s. Courtesy of Sarah Wikander.*

How Berkeley Went Dry

One morning in 1905, Mary Cartwright noticed a stranger who, like herself, was wearing a white ribbon—a fellow member of the pro-temperance "White Ribbon Army."

"Wouldn't it be a good thing," the stranger mused, "to have a prohibition clause in the new city charter?"

Why, yes it would. Cartwright stepped inside a nearby doorway that led to the office of Friend Richardson, editor of the *Berkeley Gazette*. By the time she stepped out, the *Gazette* was pushing the plan.

What is it you want?, Cartwright was asked over the next few months as she carried her crusade to the Chamber of Commerce and civic clubs throughout the city. "Just this, gentleman, that you as an influential body put yourselves on record in favor of a clause in the new charter forever prohibiting the licensing of liquor-selling in our university town."[1]

As a result of Cartwright's campaign, Berkeley got a jump on Prohibition by a good ten years, banning the sale of alcoholic beverages—but not their consumption—anywhere in town. Voters backed the measure by a three-to-one margin. "Berkeley is the largest 'dry' town in the state," the Woman's Christian Temperance Union of Northern and Central California bragged.

It had been a long fight. Berkeley had banned liquor sales a few years earlier—but now the ban had more force and would be harder to dislodge.

Thanks to the university, Berkeley had always been in the forefront of temperance. State law banned the sale of liquor within a mile of the campus in 1876. For the next century—even after the 21st Amendment ended nationwide Prohibition in 1933—the sale of hard liquor, and sometimes wine and beer as well, was banned within a mile, or at times a mile and a half, of campus.

But Berkeley was never completely dry. When drink was barred near campus, West Berkeley remained the domain of the "saloon men"—at times with more than two dozen saloons, many with gambling.[2] Dances at Sisterna Hall were awash with drink, and by 1879, Chris Johnson's Sample Room in the hall was offering "a fine assortment of wines and liquors by the flask, bottle or gallon for medicinal or family use, at city prices."[3]

Cal students in the early days had no trouble finding enough liquor to fuel "busts," which often followed an afternoon of quail shooting in the hills.

And banning booze was never enough. Enforcement was lax. Some restaurants had hidden rooms that served home brew. Others sold it in milk jugs. For years Town Trustees approved licenses for saloons, even within the one-mile limit. And juries rarely convicted the few saloon keepers whose cases made it to trial.

The Temperance Movement was more than a puritanical crusade. Many of its leaders were progressives who saw banning drink as a way to protect women and children from physical and financial ruin brought on by husbands who would deplete their moral and monetary resources at the saloon.

Many of Berkeley's leading progressives, including suffragists and J. Stitt Wilson, a preacher who would become

Places

Willard Park south of campus is named for Frances Willard, suffragist and longtime president of the Woman's Christian Temperance Union.

Berkeley's first Socialist mayor, were anti-saloon.[4] The anti-salooners took on other causes as well—white slavery, the vote for women, anti-tobacco. Frank Soulé, another Berkeley Socialist and an emeritus professor at Cal, lead the Anti-Tobacco League, which tried to ban smoking and convinced state lawmakers to ban sales to children.[5]

The anti-saloon fight took on overtones of class warfare, with university folks and businessmen in the hills coming down on the working-class saloons in the flatlands. The *Courier* accused the hill dwellers of hypocrisy. "There are hundreds of private sideboards in the fashionable district about the campus, better stocked with and carrying more numerous brands of liquors and liqueurs than any barroom in either the west or the south end," the paper editorialized.[6]

And the Woman's Christian Temperance Union got slapped after protesting when a grateful family served beer to the firefighters who had just saved their house. "Plenty of cold bottles were set forth," the *Courier* wrote. "Parched throats gratefully received the cooling beverages. Berkeley is a temperance town, but corks may pop as merrily as they choose in a private residence."[7]

And how about Bill Henderson's much-anticipated French restaurant, set to replace "the dog man," a hotdog vendor. "Just think!" the *Courier* wrote. "A French restaurant and no wine."[8]

How Berkeley Boomed

By 1905 Berkeley was becoming a city, with 23,000 people, 24 churches, 28 fraternal organizations, two hospitals, one asylum, four hotels, eleven restaurants, and eight livery stables.[1] The town was booming. "Over 600 houses within 10 months is a story few stop to appreciate properly," the *Courier* noted.[2]

Berkeley had become an all-American boomtown. But Berkeley's boom had something unique about it—something that clearly forecast the kind of town it would soon become. The developers who filled the town's hillsides and flats with homes were canny. They knew how to attract rail service and how to trumpet their wares. But they were aesthetic as well, some of them proto-environmentalists, filled with a love for nature and an interest in smart planning. Like Berkeley's Bohemians, the best of them shared a high-minded image of the good life.

By 1905, boomtown Berkeley was experiencing city problems— raw sewage in the streets and outbreaks of typhoid. "Clean up Berkeley," the paper urged. "For a town designed by nature for a living paradise, Berkeley has a very poor showing in the way of attractive streets and front yards," the paper wrote, noting downtown lots given over to four-foot thistle and "a positive stench along Shattuck Avenue after any hot day."[3]

Even the "exclusive boarding house" Cloyne Court had a courtyard filled with "old cans, coffee grounds and rotten vegetables," eliciting complaints from artist William Keith, "fearing that his dogs will eat something besides porterhouse steaks."[4]

Modern conveniences introduced modern problems. The Key Route and Southern Pacific commuter trains kicked up "sandstorms" and vibrated so much that they dislodged the brand new telephone wires.

And autos were becoming "as familiar almost as any other vehicle on the streets," the *Courier* wrote. By spring 1906, the

1907: *The Berkeley Bank of Savings rises on Shattuck Avenue in 1907. The Southern Pacific Depot is in the center of the street. Courtesy of the Berkeley Historical Society, 113.190.3417.*

Courier claimed, Berkeley was "an Auto Town," with fifty-nine cars owned by residents and eighteen by businesses—with three available for rent. "According to population, this is the banner automobile town outside of Los Angeles."[5]

Along with cars came drivers, including "the scorcher," the notorious Mr. Ramsey, "the most reckless driver in town."[6] Ramsey did have competition, however, including the grocer who was brought to task for the "fiery broncos on his delivery wagons."[7]

Then came the San Francisco earthquake of April 18, 1906, and Berkeley really boomed, becoming the fastest-growing city in the state and one of the fastest in the country as refugees flooded to town via ferry. Many liked what they saw and stayed. Berkeley's population zoomed from 13,214 in 1900 to 56,000 in 1920.

Berkeley was filled with hillside neighborhoods of curved "pleasure drives," ample landscaping, rose-colored sidewalks, and rustic paths. The rock outcroppings of North Berkeley were preserved in backyards, alongside houses, or as small pocket parks.

Houses, mostly stucco-sided and a surprising number of quaint Storybooks, were designed by talented architects like John Hudson Thomas, Walter Ratcliff, and John Galen Howard. Duncan McDuffie, one of the leading developers, was an avid Sierra hiker, a Sierra Club president, and a founder of the East Bay Park system. He also led a campaign in 1908 to turn Berkeley into the state capital, offering a perfect site surrounded by streets named after the counties. The scheme was rejected by a statewide vote.

1900s: *The Bear Fountain at Marin Circle was designed by developer Duncan McDuffie and associates to form an ensemble including the state capitol. John Galen Howard designed the fountain and sculptor Arthur Putnam designed the bears. Postcard courtesy of Sarah Wikander.*

"This fair domain is so to be developed as to conserve its native charm and cause each home-maker's work to enhance the beauty of the whole. Intelligent cooperation, a pre-figured plan, a community spirit, and an artistic and enlight-ened forethought will make Claremont," the McDuffie Co. wrote about one of its neighborhoods, "a lesson to home-building America."[8]

And so it did.

How Berkeley Pioneered Modern Crime Fighting

Thieves "have learned that they can work in this city without molestation by the police," the *Gazette* reported in 1903, citing a recent jewelry heist at the home of Mr. and Mrs. Morgan. "Realizing that it was useless to ask the local police to apprehend the marauders, the Morgans telephoned the occurrence to the Oakland department."[1]

"Strictly speaking," the *Courier* wrote in 1905, "the town has no police force."[2] There was one marshal and four officers, none of them professionally trained. For a time, none of them worked at night.

That all changed in 1905, when August Vollmer—a Marine veteran of the Spanish-American War's bloody Philippines campaign, and a town firefighter—was elected marshal. He was already a local hero for averting disaster when a loose railcar threatened to plow into a passenger train.

c. 1910: *August Vollmer, center, with his College Cops. Courtesy of the Berkeley Historical Society, 433.191.2134.*

1900: *Walter Gordon, shown with his wife, Elizabeth, captained the Wonder Team for a season, became Berkeley's first black policeman, and then went on to become governor of the Virgin Islands. Courtesy of the Bancroft Library of the University of California, Berkeley.*

The twenty-five-year-old "boy marshal" looked silly when he raided several Chinese opium dens and found himself in court "up against the old difficulty of being unable to identify the Chinamen," the *Courier* wrote.[3]

And Vollmer's face turned red at a party during his first months in office. Surrounded by a gaggle of pretty girls, Vollmer decided to show off his handcuffs—snapping them around one miss's wrist—before realizing he didn't have the key.[4]

But Vollmer wised up. Although he claimed to have no education, education is what he based his policing on. That, plus technology and science—sometimes, pseudo-science. By 1906, Berkeley had its first bicycle patrol, a centralized record system that tracked criminals' modi operandi, and a system of electric lights spaced throughout town to communicate with officers. It was said to be the first electric police communications system in the country.

By 1913, Berkeley had the earliest all-motorized police department in the nation, and by 1919, the city equipped some of its cars with radios. In 1915, Berkeley had its own crime detection lab.

Vollmer subjected would-be recruits to intelligence tests and, in 1908, started the Berkeley Police School—also a first. By 1917, the school—run with the university —taught physics, chemistry, biology, "criminology, anthropology and heredity," and "criminological psychology." The force was known nationwide as "Berkeley's College Cops."[5]

A fan of Cesar Lombroso, who believed criminals could be identified by such characteristics as large jaws, Vollmer provided instruction on "race degeneration," "eugenics," and "hereditary crime and criminal tendencies." Students learned about such "indirect factors" in crime as saloons, gambling, prostitution, "dime novels," and "daily papers." They also learned about preventing crime through education, art, sanitation, and "intelligent police."

"Criminologists know that a policeman's energies should be devoted to removing causes of crime, not to pursuing criminals," Vollmer said. "But the average policeman doesn't know that."[6]

Places

Vollmer Peak in Tilden Regional Park is named for the chief. You can catch Leonarde Keeler playing himself in the film Call Northside 777.

"We must deal with the child in the early and plastic period of his life, when his attitudes, his religious, social and personal ideals are being developed," he told the *Gazette* in 1930. Vollmer sent policewomen into Berkeley schools to inculcate the young.[7]

One of the first lie detectors was developed in Berkeley by John A. Larsen, a PhD in physiology whom Vollmer brought to the department. The machine was improved in 1920 by Leonarde Keeler, the son of Berkeley poet Charles Keeler, who was a friend of the chief.

Eloise Keeler, Leonarde's sister, watched as seventeen-year-old "Narde" first tried out his machine, "a strange contraption consisting of tubes, wires, glass bulb and a wide strip of black smoked paper which moved." The "suspect" was Eloise's best friend Chickie.

"Do you love Charlie?" Narde asked. "The needles recording Chickie's blood pressure and breathing had suddenly lurched."

"It's true. I do have a kind of crush on Charlie."

Eloise revealed why Vollmer was interested in such a machine: "The chief would not tolerate third-degree methods such as beating with a rubber hose."[8]

"The Keeler Polygraph" became one of the most used in the country, and Leonarde became a leading criminologist.

Vollmer, "an iron-gray man," *Colliers* magazine said, "with iron in his face and gray in his hair," opposed capital punishment and treated panhandlers leniently. Police officers, he said, need to possess "moral impregnability." He also believed in free speech, backing the YMCA's decision to open its meeting rooms to everyone, even Communists, a philosophy he had no truck with. Believers in Socialism, Bolshevism, and "WWI-ism" he consigned to the "paranoiac" and "mentally twisted" personality types.

By 1924, according to *Colliers* magazine, Vollmer was "the most famous policeman in the world."[9]

Vollmer, who retired as chief in 1932, continued teaching at the university until 1937. He remained active in the community, helping create the East Bay Regional Park District. In 1955, near blind and suffering from cancer and Parkinson's disease, he took his own life after telling his housekeeper, "Call the Berkeley Police. I'm going to shoot myself."[10]

How Berkeley Pioneered Women's Rights

Mary McHenry chafed in 1875 when other coeds went gaga over a cute new professor, historian Bernard Moses. "At that time I was fully determined, or thought I was, never to marry," she told a reporter for the *Berkeley Gazette* years later. She also objected to the way he taught—he asked women the easy questions.

"When I was younger than I am now," she said, "I blamed man indiscriminately for the unjust condition of woman's life."[1]

McHenry, a judge's daughter, did marry shortly after graduating from Cal's law school in 1882—choosing the artist William Keith. McHenry worked briefly as a lawyer; "special attention paid to probate business," her card read.[2] But it was only after becoming Mary McHenry Keith that her lifework started.

By the early 1890s, she was one of the leading fighters for women's rights in California, lecturing on behalf of the Political Equality Club of Alameda County and leading an excursion to the top of Mt. Tam with Susan B. Anthony.

1890s: *Mary McHenry Keith, one of the West Coast's leading suffragists, at home with Jumbo and Hegel. Courtesy of the Bancroft Library of the University of California, Berkeley.*

c. 1910: *Leola Hall, left, was a suffragist leader and a self-taught architect. She's driving to a rally, c.1910. Courtesy of the Berkeley Historical Society, 490-191-5354.*

In 1896, the year California voters rejected statewide suffrage for women, Mary sat with a reporter from the *Gazette*. "William Keith, the man I know best, is my ideal," she said, "for he doesn't care how often women vote if they will only let him paint."[3]

In 1902, when the *Gazette* visited again, Mary was president of the Berkeley Political Equality Society. "Mrs. Keith is a dainty little blue-eyed, rosy woman, whose gray hair is a good many years in advance of her face and still further ahead of her heart. Somehow she doesn't suggest suffrage in the least," the paper said. "You can't, when chatting with her in her artistic little parlor, imagine her presiding over a meeting of 'long-haired men and short-haired women.' "

"Mrs. Keith keeps a club of two hundred suffragists going over in Berkeley. It is the largest suffrage club on the coast.

"The fact is, she is not at all fierce on the subject of her theories, but she has the knack for coaxing people over to her way of thinking. The most determined of anti-suffrage women give in to her . . . her husband gives in to her."[4]

Women were playing a larger role in the Berkeley community—and it was not to everyone's liking. At the start of 1905, the *Courier* reported with amusement that Berkeley women had formed a political club to block a proposed boulevard.

"What effect the work of these will have is one that is problematic. Some say that the influence of mothers, wives and sweethearts over sons, husbands and fiancés respectively will cause a political landslide," the *Courier* observed. "Some appear to be amused and say that husbands have too much knowledge of women kind to be swayed in matters outside of the family domicile, and some sneer and make unkind remarks about women of uncertain age who have got beyond the period where either husbands or sweethearts are possible, and that such influence need not be feared."[5]

In 1906, the city charter was amended to allow women to vote on school issues—and only school issues—and to serve on the school board. By 1907, Mary's Political Equality Society had won over the Chamber of Commerce. In 1911, voters finally approved women's suffrage in California. Berkeley voted 2,417 yea, 1,761 nay. All the voters, of course, were men.

How Berkeley Trod the Boards

Sam Hume

Sam Hume, *in character. Courtesy of the Bancroft Library of the University of California, Berkeley.*

"The King and the Booster" made quite a splash as presented by the Class of 1908. Onstage, among the cast of sixty-two, were "Violontra, the princess of Palenthia," and her nemesis, "Evil Genius Number One." Adding to the din were a demon chorus, a Teddy Bear chorus, an Amazon chorus—and "an automobile chorus."[1]

The audience roared at the entry of "Reginald Ruffnecke Rahrah," as performed by the show's coauthor, Sam Hume. He had taken center stage in Berkeley and for the next five decades did his best to stay there. Like Charles Keeler, he made himself an exemplar of the good life as lived through art and was as Berkeley a character as you can find in any decade of the city's existence. A political liberal who fought against anti-Asian discrimination, he promoted the arts as the answer to all of man's ills.

Hume, who won fame in the 1910s for running the university's Greek Theatre, was far from Berkeley's first impresario. Theater—from vaudeville to Shakespeare—was on the boards from the start, from performances at Sisterna Hall in Ocean View to touring productions at Harmon Gymnasium, which opened on campus in 1879.

By 1900, the Berkeley Opera House was presenting such troupes as the Edward B. Adonis Big Vaudeville Co., with Stanley & Scheaffer "in a laughable sketch entitled Mrs. O'Grady's Washday. Note—a thrilling slack wire act performed in this sketch."[2]

The Greek Theatre, which opened in 1903, was the first open-air Greek amphitheater in the United States, emphasizing Berkeley's nickname, the Athens of the West. It became a major venue, featuring such performers as Sarah Bernhardt. But the Greek really came into its own in 1918 when Hume took charge. Besides Greek drama, classics, and modern works by Shaw and O'Neill, Hume used the Greek for pageants, with hundreds of students and townspeople onstage in togas.

Hume brought to Berkeley such professionals as Irving Pichel and George Pierce Baker, who founded Berkeley Playmakers, an innovative Little Theater. By 1930, Playmakers was teaching theater to high schoolers and running an annual Little Theater Tournament featuring troupes from around the bay. Pichel, who went on to become a Hollywood director and actor ("Sandor" in *Dracula's Daughter*) was also the son-in-law of Berkeley's Socialist mayor, J. Stitt Wilson.

Playmakers died around 1940. "It's rotten the Playmakers should have such financial worries," Eugene O'Neill wrote the troupe, while declining to send money.[3]

In 1924, Hume left the university but continued to prosper. He and his second wife, Portia Bell Hume (she later became a prominent psychiatrist and a sculptor), had Berkeley architect John Hudson Thomas create the town's most unique dwelling—which is saying something—a medieval cloister complete with courtyard and tower.

Places

Hume Cloister can be spotted at 2900 Buena Vista Way, uphill from Maybeck country.

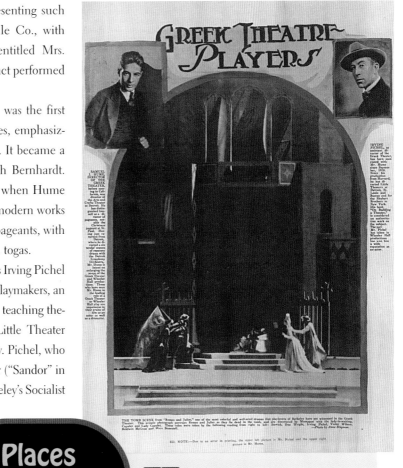

Hume, *left, and Irving Pichel, right, appear on a poster for Hume's Greek Theatre Players. Courtesy of the Bancroft Library of the University of California, Berkeley.*

In 1925, Hume visited Massachusetts to produce *Lexington*, which a Boston paper called "America's Passion Play of Civil Liberty."[4]

Two years later he was in Paris, rounding up films "devoted

c. 1910s: *A toga-clad procession at the Greek Theatre emphasizes Berkeley's claim to be "the Athens of the Pacific." Postcard courtesy of Sarah Wikander.*

to special foreign pictures" for what he envisioned as a chain of small cinemas in the States.[5] Soon Hume was showing films in San Francisco and planning Berkeley's first off-campus art museum, the Berkeley Art Museum.

The museum, which opened in 1929 on Shattuck Avenue, showed Tibetan paintings, Alexander Jawlensky, and Franz Marc. Hume planned a building with three galleries, a junior museum, and a large oval theater. But in 1932, the Depression did the museum in.

The late twenties were a busy time for Hume. In 1928, he published what became a standard work on stagecraft, *Twentieth Century Stage Design*. He also emerged as California's state-appointed czar of leisure. As "director of avocational education," Hume's job was to teach Californians "how to use their newfound leisure."[6] Or, as one headline put it, "Hume heads new department that will seek cure for 'Jazz Mania.' "[7]

Hume's cure, much like Charles Keeler's Cosmic Religion, sought moral regeneration through the arts. He reached the public through the still-new medium of radio. "The machine age tends to make robots of us all," he said. "This is why we have more neurotics in the United States than anywhere else in the world."[8]

In the mid-'30s, Hume was a force behind the California Council on Oriental Relations, whose goal was to end the Chinese Exclusion Act and to "attempt to counteract the poisonous propaganda . . . flooding our press designed to create fear of Japanese."[9]

After the war, Hume raised great Danes, spent time with Portia on a ranch near Healdsburg, and ran a bookstore and art gallery in Berkeley called At the Sign of the Palindrome, which became a hangout for writers and artists. Hume died in 1962. Like many of Berkeley's greats, he had large ambitions—to remake modern stagecraft, to create museum and film palaces, to be America's Max Reinhardt—that he never accomplished.

But Hume set the pace for theater in Berkeley, which remains vital and innovative. Among troupes that made Berkeley home have been the Blake Street Hawkeyes (a collective founded in 1973), the long-running Berkeley Repertory Theater, the Aurora Theater, and the satirical Culture Clash.

1970s: *Cynthia Moore, Whoopi Goldberg, Bob Ernst, and David Schein made up one contingent of the Blake Street Hawkeyes. Courtesy of the Berkeley Historical Society. Photo by Allen Nomura.*

2000: *The theater troupe Culture Clash, which specializes in hilarious Chicano political satire, developed its chops at Berkeley's La Peña cultural center. Courtesy of La Peña.*

How Berkeley Went Socialist

Mayor J. Stitt Wilson

Today, outsiders may call Berkeley "the People's Republic." During its early twentieth-century heyday, however, the city was run primarily by Republicans. But Berkeleyans—even then—were not immune to the call of the Socialists for a more equable divvying of life's spoils.

In 1911, when Socialist J. Stitt Wilson ran for mayor, even a paper not known for its radical opinions supported his cause. "His well-rounded sentences, polished rhetoric and telling logic drove home the truth with great power," the *Gazette* said of his kickoff speech.[1]

Wilson, then a boyish forty-three, called for public ownership of lighting and electricity, streetcars, water and phones, and a public kindergarten, with all these services provided at minimal cost. The battle, he said, set private citizens versus "a mere handful of individuals who control the resources of the nation."[2] Wilson, a backer of women's suffrage, already had the support of Berkeley's progressive women.

"You know what I am standing for," he said to rousing cheers, "cheaper water, cheaper gas, cheaper lights, cheaper phones."[3]

It was five years before the Bolshevik Revolution, and "Socialism" had yet to become a dirty word. The years before the Great War were a high time for Socialists in America, with seventy or so cities electing Socialist mayors, and Eugene Debs, the perennial presidential candidate, providing the party with a charismatic face.

Wilson, once a Canadian preacher, made his name in town in 1905 as a leader of the Berkeley Anti-Vaccination League.

Wilson took the stump against small pox vaccinations, claiming they caused disease. He did so effectively. "Vaccination an evil," the *Courier* trumpeted in a headline.[4]

His socialist exhortations often took on biblical overtones. Consider his lecture "The Barbary Coast in a Barbarous Land: Or the Harlots and the Pharisees." "Prostitution," he intoned, "is the rotten pus running out of your respectable, legalized church-sanctioned capitalist system of industry."[5]

As mayor—he won by a mere 281 votes—Wilson fought his first battle with his own party. The Socialists required its members to sign resignation papers upon taking office and put them in the hands of the party so it could turn those out of office who disobeyed its edicts. Wilson told them to take a hike.[6]

When folks in West Berkeley complained about fire danger because of a lack of water, in two days Wilson made sure they had access to a water tank.

His ally on the city council, John A. Wilson, proposed to ban smoking in any "restaurant, waiting room, office, store, streetcar or any other place used by the public"—a measure whose time didn't come for another ninety years. "Berkeley smokers who like to take a puff of the fragrant weed are in for the most uncomfortable time of their lives," the *Independent* warned.[7]

Another failed initiative was the mayor's plan to build a municipal lighting plant. Wilson and city attorney Redmond ("Reddy") Staats also failed in their attempt to block the merger of Home Telephone and Pacific States Telephone companies.

Wilson didn't mind making enemies. When the realty men asked the city to ease their tax burden, he faced them at a public meeting and said, "A laundryman is more valuable to the community than a real estate man."[8]

By 1912, Wilson was ready for bigger things—Congress. His chances looked good. After all, he'd pulled in 12 percent of the votes in his try for governor in 1910. The *Berkeley Independent* got into his corner, painting incumbent Joe

Big Mass Meeting

IN SCOTTISH RITE AUDITORIUM
Sutter Street and Van Ness Avenue
San Francisco

Tuesday, October 24th
AT 8 O'CLOCK P. M.

Under Auspices of DISTRICT LODGE NO. 7, I. O. G. T.

HON.

J. STITT WILSON
EX-MAYOR OF BERKELEY

Will Speak on

"CALIFORNIA WET OR DRY"

ADMISSION FREE

Knowland as a pawn of the monopolists and the trusts, and printing Wilson's exhortations in their entirety.

Wilson's program for the United States much resembled his program for Berkeley: collective ownership of rail, wire, wireless, phone, mines, quarries, oil wells, forests, water power, steamboats, stockyards, "and all large-scale industries."[9]

He called for the conservation of timber, the reclamation of swamps and the creation of new highways and waterways. The Supreme Court should no longer be allowed to overturn legislation. Children under sixteen shouldn't work. The work-week should be shortened to six and a half days, and there

1900s: *J. Stitt Wilson, Berkeley's first Socialist mayor, also hit the lecture circuit on behalf of temperance. Courtesy of the Bancroft Library of the University of California, Berkeley.*

should be a minimum wage.

Knowland won by 9,100 votes. Wilson lost his hometown by 419 votes. Wilson, who chose not to run for reelection in 1913, ran unsuccessfully as a Socialist for Congress in 1932 and for governor in 1936 and 1940.

Berkeley had to wait sixty-six years—till Gus Newport in 1979—to have another socialist (small "s" this time) mayor.

How Berkeley Caught the Flu

Berkeley was a magical place for Agnes Edwards, who entered as a freshman in 1917, after growing up in the backwater town of Brawley in the broiling Imperial Valley. The freshman rally really got to her. "The yells simply made your spine tingle," she wrote.[1]

And she loved the Pajamarino Rally, with students in pajamas snaking their way uphill to the Greek Theatre. There, with spotlights glowing off the Golden Bear above the stage and with red-white-and-blue banners fluttering, students sang patriotic songs and enjoyed a bonfire and fireworks. Seniors were dressed like soldiers and sailors—and many soon became soldiers and sailors.

The United States was entering the Great War. By October 1918, thirty-five hundred students and faculty were in the military and at least forty-five had died. Agnes grieved for a friend who was killed in France and worried about her doughboy brother.

The campus provided preflight training for three thousand men through its School for Military Aeronautics. Barracks were built and a Students Army Training Corps established. In 1918, the Blue and Gold yearbook reported that the university opened late for the first time, "with its honored and beloved Golden Bear replaced by a more honored and revered emblem—the Eagle."

Anti-German feeling was strong—except with President Wheeler, who had studied at Heidelberg and knew the Kaiser. Art professor Eugen Neuhaus, an émigré who never lost his German accent, got along well. "Although there was at least one faculty member who was sure I had been placed here by the German government as a spy. Hadn't I painted nearly the whole coast of California?"[2]

"The number of engagements and marriages among the students is awful—every day the 'Cal' has a half dozen or more announcements," Agnes wrote her folks. "The war seems to be hurrying things along."

Complicating all of this was the Spanish influenza epidemic, which killed twenty to forty million worldwide, hitting Berkeley in October 1918 and then returning there in January. More than fourteen hundred caught the flu on campus and more in the city. The disease hit quickly with chills, an aching fever, nausea, dizziness, and weakness. Often it passed—but often it killed. By mid-November, Berkeley had 2,251 cases and one hundred had died.

The city council banned public gatherings and ordered residents to wear gauze masks, with failure punishable by a $500 fine or ten days in jail. Many ignored the law. Dean of women Lucy Stebbins and student volunteers, including Agnes, made the masks, which Agnes called the "craziest looking things."

The *Gazette* played the menace down, burying the story low on page one or inside. "Allies smash foe on three fronts" and "Yanks cross Meuse in sudden smash" were typical top-of-the-page heads.

Through it all, Agnes—certainly as sensible a coed as the university has seen—kept up a full load of studies, attended every dance, entertained sailors who were based on Goat Island, worked several increasingly responsible jobs as stenographer and a manager at the university, played in the mandolin and guitar club, and wrote her parents close to a letter a day.

"Don't worry about me catching the influenza," she wrote, even though the minister of her church had just died of it, as well as seven students. "The kids call it the *floo* or the *flooey*.

"Everything is closed—schools, churches, movies, etc. All the boys are either sick or in quarantine, so there's absolutely nothing happening." Even though she attended a school where most of the "men" were freshmen, Agnes made do with the aviators, whom she found were "the swellest dancers."

"I had a peach of a time—best time I've had for ages because they were all so wide awake and are *real* men. These college fellows mostly act bored to death most of the time."

Agnes got to hear the first-ever playing of the new Berkeley Campanile's chimes. "They certainly have a beautiful tone too, so mellow and deep. The fellow that played them wasn't much good, tho."

She also got to celebrate Armistice. "The siren on the power plant blew for about two hours & yes, the fire department was out, and everyone had horns and cowbells, and the girls went down and got our Chinese gong, and pounded and

pounded . . . When the Campanile chimes began to play the national airs of all the Allies, we really began to celebrate."

1900: *Employees of Cutter labs in West Berkeley donned masks during the flu epidemic. Courtesy of the Oakland Museum of California.*

How Berkeley Burned

In many ways, 1923 was a good year in Berkeley. The city inaugurated its progressive, city-manager form of government. An auto-ferry between Berkeley and San Francisco started service, providing an alternative to the regular commute via the Oakland ferries. The publicly owned East Bay Municipal Utility District formed to provide better water than earlier private companies; within a few years, it would be piping snowmelt straight from the Sierra.

But it was also the year Berkeley burned.

Did people sense it coming? Perhaps. "Freakish heat hits bay," the *Chronicle* reported, "one of the hottest winds ever recorded in this region."[1]

The hot, dry wind blew across Berkeley on September 16 from bone-dry valleys to the east. "All through the night, the hot gale swept across the city, dry as ashes and laden with a murky fragrance like incense," according to a pamphlet titled "Berkeley Fire 1923," published soon after. "People fell asleep listening to the

1923: *Berkeley's Northside, once among its finest neighborhoods, lay in ruins a few days after the fire. Courtesy of the Berkeley Historical Society, 5.1.192 1018.*

rustle of the dried leaves that scuttled endlessly along the empty streets—unheeded messengers of disaster."[2]

Shortly after 2 p.m. on September 17, in her open-air Temple of the Wings, dancer Florence Boynton saw smoke rise over the top of the Berkeley Hills. "That fire is miles back in the hills, way out of our jurisdiction," the fire department told her when she called. "Don't worry, Mrs. Boynton, don't worry."[3]

But Berkeley's first family of Bohemians took no chances. Daughter Sulgwynn grabbed her best clothes, the heirlooms, and her canary, "just a quiet, sweet little bird," and got out. The bird was motionless. The Temple was one of the first houses to burn.

A 1,600-foot-wide wall of flame, which began near a hiking trail in Wildcat Canyon, raced down the hillsides toward downtown. Forestry experts later blamed smokers.

"The sun swam as a diminished ball of blood behind the streaming veil of smoke," the pamphlet "Berkeley Fire 1923" recounted. "From the region of the fire came a roar like that of a great cataract."

As people fled down the hill—on foot, in cars, carrying possessions, crying—firefighters did their best. But there was no water pressure. The next day the *Gazette* reported that by 4 p.m., the firefighters tried dynamite to remove fuel, "checking the flames for a few moments."[4]

One after the other, houses, apartment buildings, and churches caught fire. "Nails in the houses in the path of the fire melted before they were touched," the pamphlet said. "Buildings seemed to explode and flounder in an instantaneous dissolution."

Meanwhile, ferries were scurrying across the bay—not carrying Berkeleyans to San Francisco, as they had carried San Franciscans to Berkeley after the 1906 quake, but instead bringing sightseers from the city.[5]

Cal football players raced to the home of former president Benjamin Ide Wheeler, saving his art collection and some of his books and furniture. Wheeler, touched, "passed around the cigars," the *Chronicle* said.[6]

Maybeck's daughter, Kerna, saved a neighbor's house, which was designed by her father, by beating out the sparks. The Theta Chi fraternity house, "in the very center of the fire," was saved by a bucket brigade of students. "The house seemed almost a certain victim to the flames," the *Chronicle* reported, "but sixty students, working like so many veteran firemen, combated the sweeping menace—and won."[7]

Hundreds of students risked their lives fighting the fire or rescuing victims. Robert E. Hill, alerted by a sorority girl that her grandmother was in danger, "rushed to the scene, carried the aged woman on his back to the yard. Finding the family automobile in the garage he lifted her into it and sped through streets aflame on either side," the *Chronicle* reported. "The top of the car was burned and a tire exploded from the heat, it is said. He collapsed following the rescue, but was resuscitated shortly."[8]

Not everyone was selfless. Two young men offered to help Mrs. A. M. McCoy, who had just loaded her car with $10,000 worth of jewels, oriental rugs, and treasures from Europe. Instead, they made off with it.[9]

What really stopped the fire is what started it—the wind. The loss: 584 buildings destroyed, thirty or more damaged.

Recriminations focused on the lack of water and water pressure. But "Berkeley Fire 1923" wasn't buying it. "The water supply may have been inadequate, but rivers of water could have been poured into that blaze without deterring it."

The toll: one of Berkeley's most beautiful neighborhoods, with homes designed by Maybeck and other fine architects, was almost entirely destroyed. Scientists lost research, writers their manuscripts. Libraries and art collections were destroyed. Eleanor Carlisle, one of Berkeley's grandest dames, a feminist activist and conservationist, lost her home and collection of Chinese art. Thousands were left homeless.

But no lives were lost—despite reports that filled the papers for days of students who died fighting the fire. Several students were badly injured. Doctors and nurses who raced to the campus to tend to the injured found themselves with little to do. Even Sulgwynn's canary pulled through. "It lived a long time after that," she said. "It sang beautifully."[10]

Three days after the fire the *Chronicle* reported that the Temple of the Wings was one of the "earliest worms" to start the "rebuilding game." The top headline: "The renaissance of stricken Berkeley began yesterday."[11]

Sixty-eight years later, another great fire burned through the East Bay Hills. The Oakland Hills fire of 1991 only torched a relatively small portion of the southern Berkeley Hills and destroyed whole neighborhoods in Oakland. It reminded people that living amongst nature has its risks.

How Berkeley Won the Big Game

T he first real encouragement given by anyone to athletic sports at the University, is the improvement of a ball ground on a portion of the University domain," the *Berkeley Advocate* wrote at the start of 1878. "Let attention be kept directed to the physical man, and possibly some day there will be a definite system of muscle culture established at our University, as the equally important and concomitant sister of mental training."[1]

Over the years, muscle culture had its ups and downs at Cal, from Roy Riegel's 73-yard wrong-way run in the 1929 Rose Bowl (Berkeley lost 8–7) to The Play against Stanford in 1982—a kickoff and five laterals that had the Bears charging to victory through the Stanford band, which had taken to the field prematurely.

Cal has had fabulous track - and-field teams, and at various times has been a national force in rugby, swimming, water polo, basketball, and crew. And it was baseball that gave Cal one of its most notorious traditions—the Battle for the Axe, which is now the official trophy of the annual Big Game of football between Cal and Stanford.

It was April 1899 at a baseball field in San Francisco, with a cold wind blowing. Close to seven hundred Bear rooters filled the stands. Spirits remained high after the Bears' 9–7 victory—when E. J. Brown and friends spied "a large battle axe" that had been ground sharp and brought to the game by Stanford rooters. It was Cal's Carl Hayden who grabbed it, the *Daily Cal* reported, pursued by half a dozen Stanford men.

Soon "there was a running skirmish for a mile or more." The axe was passed from man to man, "the handle cut off and the blade given to Clinton Miller, the only one who had an overcoat. The crowd then boarded a car to the San Francisco pier.

1899: *Cal students march through campus carrying the Stanford axe the day after capturing it. Courtesy of the Bancroft Library of the University of California, Berkeley.*

Awaiting the Bears at the pier, however, was the law. What to do? "When almost at their wits' ends, a young lady friend of Miller's passed the group. With a sudden inspiration, he said good-bye to the others, walked up to the young lady, and passed through the ferry gate with her without being questioned."[2]

A brave move indeed, but it pales next to the story of Cal's first Wonder Team, a football squad that from 1920 to 1925—never lost a game. Coach Andy Smith became a campus legend, as did players Brick Muller ("the big redhead") and Duke Morrison.[3]

The team was particularly challenged because, from 1906 to 1915, Cal hadn't played "American football," but rugby. President Benjamin Ide Wheeler despised football as "a spectacle and not a sport."

"Two rigid ramparts-like lines of human flesh have been created," Wheeler wrote, "one of defense, the other of offense, and behind the latter is established a catapult to fire through a porthole opened in the defensive ramparts a missile composed of four or five human bodies globulated about a carried football against the presumably weakest part in the opposition rampart. The 'part' is a single human being. The participants in the game are not players but cogs in a machine. Each man does one thing over and over."[4]

It didn't take long for Cal to get back into football, however, once Smith came on as assistant coach in 1916 and then head coach a year later. By 1921, thirty thousand people were attending games.

Smith was loved for his modesty and humor as well as his skill. He always wore the same dilapidated hat—until he found a note stuck in its band: "For Gods sake, throw this lid away."[5] His players gave him a new one. After a writer dubbed them "the Wonder Team," Smith protested, "You're ruining my team!"[6]

In 1922, the campus convulsed with excitement as the Stanford game approached. The team sponsored a smoker rally, complete with two orchestras, boxing matches, and ten thousand Chesterfield cigarettes provided to all comers by Liggett and Meyers. "Even the dense smoke choking every corner of Harmon

Places

Memorial Stadium, "the House Andy Built," opened for play in 1923.

Gymnasium could not blot or blur our fighting California spirit," the *Daily Cal* said.[7]

It was all worth it. "Nearly every time the ball was snapped something breathtaking happened," the *Daily Cal*'s Don Wiley wrote of the game, "and the fifty-five thousand persons who witnessed the contest were several times on the verge of heart failure."[8]

The streak snapped in 1925 with a loss to the Olympic Club—which imported many of its players from the fabled East Coast! Shortly after, while contemplating another contract with Cal, Smith died of pulmonary pneumonia. His ashes were scattered over Memorial Stadium.

"Even nature seemed to mourn," Fred Foy wrote in the *Daily Cal.* "In the morning precisely at the hour of the services, a chilling fog swept in and enveloped all assembled. As the services proceeded and Andy's praises were sung, the sun broke through and when the ashes were released from the plane they sifted gently through a warm and welcoming sky."[9]

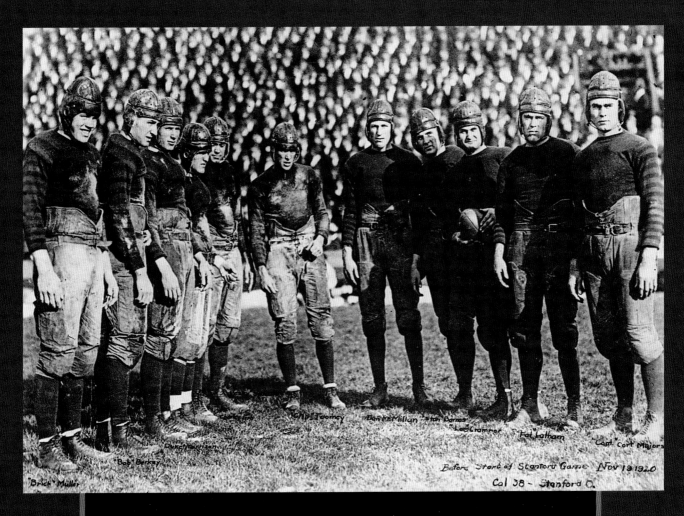

"Brick" Muller   "Bob" Berkey   Duke Morrison   Charlie Erb   Cort   "Chips" Toomey   Dan McMillan "Stan Barnes   Les Cramner   "Fat" Latham   "Capt." Cort Majors

Before Start of Stanford Game   Nov 13 1920
Cal 38 – Stanford 0.

1920s: *The Wonder Team, ready to face Stanford in 1920. "Brick" Muller is on the far left. The score? 38–0, Cal. Courtesy of the Bancroft Library of the University of California, Berkeley.*

How Berkeley
Seemed Ideal

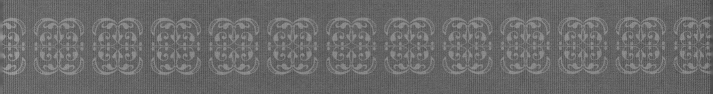

How Berkeley Spurned Spanking

In the 1920s and 1930s, Berkeley was a dream city," George A. Pettitt wrote in the mid-1970s, several years after it had devolved into what many old-timers regarded as a nightmare.[1] Back then, Pettitt wrote, it was a town of well-tended neighborhoods, good schools, parks, and public transportation. Berkeley was a predominantly white middle-class community with a conservative paper, the *Gazette,* and a city government dominated by downtown Republican merchants. Complacent. Self-satisfied. It was a city where no one slept in downtown doorways and a city that had never been tear-gassed by federal troops.

Between the world wars, Berkeley seemed to many of its inhabitants a paradise—especially in retrospect. It was consistently rated as one of the best-governed and most-livable cities in the nation. And, despite its Republican-dominated administration, the city was also in many ways a model progressive town.

It wasn't until the end of World War II when, in Pettitt's view, the dream ended, that problems ignored during the dream period surfaced—racial segregation, a poisoned industrialized waterfront, and poverty. By that time, the Republican decades were drawing to a close.

It might appear that the artistic and intellectual excitement that coursed through so much of Berkeley's society rarely found its way into municipal governance before the 1960s. But that's not so.

From the city's start, Cal professors got deeply involved with city government. William Carey Jones, founder of the law school, helped devise one of the city's charters. Professors helped the city establish one of the earliest planning departments in the state, "to provide for and regulate the future growth and development of Berkeley."[2] In 1923, Berkeley took the progressive step of adopting a council-manager form of government.

And city government came with a sense of humor. The 1927–28 annual report was written like a newspaper, complete with snappy headlines. "Useless to lose anything in Berkeley," was one. "There is simply no use in trying to lose anything in Berkeley," the item began, announcing that police chief Vollmer reported $34,611 in lost items during the year, with $32,147 of that recovered—a rate of 92.8 percent!

And, good Republican that it was, the city guarded its pocketbook, balancing revenues and expenses not just year-to-year but month-to-month. "We pay cash," a headline read in the 1935–36 report. "Since the inception of the Council-Manager plan the city has kept strictly on a cash basis and has never borrowed a penny. Considerable savings are made by virtue of this position."[3]

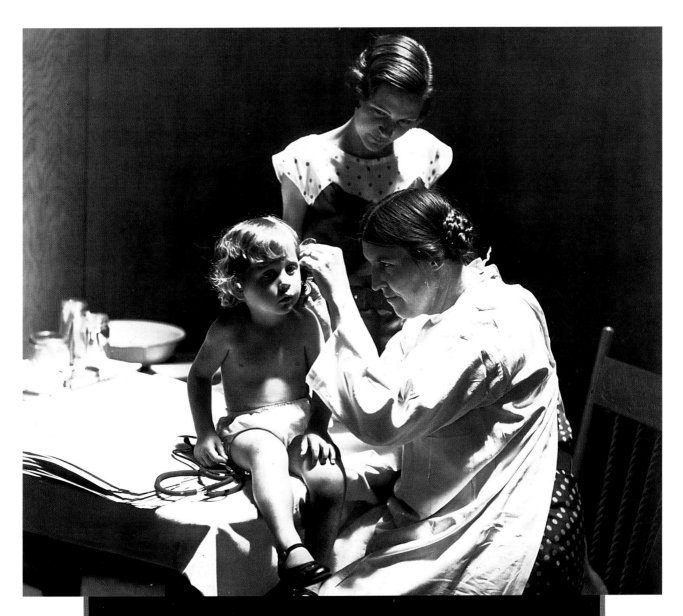

1920: *A public health nurse examines a Berkeley preschooler. Courtesy of the Berkeley Historical Society.*

Berkeley, during the inter-war years, can come across as almost a parody of a small town burg. In 1919, in the wake of Russia's Bolshevik revolution and anarchist agitation in the United States, the council passed what it called one of the strictest "red flag laws" on the West Coast, threatening fines and jail for anyone displaying "any red flag, banner or pennant," "or any sign, symbol or standard tending to promote anarchy or revolution."[4]

And in 1927, the mayor bragged about another Berkeley "first" — "an ordinance making Etiquette of the Flag a law in Berkeley."[5]

But it was in public health that Berkeley made its greatest innovations as one of the first and only cities in the state with its own public health department, one that was remarkably caring.

Although public health in Berkeley goes back to 1880 with the hiring of its first public health officer, the effort really got rolling when volunteer nurses, doctors, and laypeople banded together after the San Francisco earthquake of 1906 to help refugees, forming such groups as the Berkeley Relief Committee, the Women's Benevolent Society, and the Visiting Nurses. The University Infirmary, now the University Health Service, was also founded after the earthquake. It was the first university health service of its kind in the country.

By 1908, Berkeley had a nonprofit Day Nursery offering what was essentially municipal daycare. It was one of the first cities in the country to offer such an ambitious childcare program. Attached to the nursery was the Berkeley Health Center, which provided free health care for children and parenting classes for their moms. By 1931, 1,318 children were using daycare annually.

Places

The Day Nursery, a charming building by architect Walter Rattcliff Jr., is at 2031 Sixth Street.

With funding from the community chest and the city, and advice and staffing from the university, by the 1920s Berkeley's clinic was treating Berkeleyans who couldn't afford private care. Children who called in sick to school could expect a call from a visiting nurse, who also visited adults when necessary. In January 1924, a typical month, nurses made 171 house calls.[6]

"No baby in Berkeley need start the journey of life without the best guidance that modern science can give him," the president of the health center's auxiliary boasted.[7] The result? In 1930, Berkeley's infant mortality rate was 3 percent, versus 6 percent for the state as a whole. And when kids needed their tonsils out, ladies from the Soroptimists ferried them to the doctor.

In a small city like Berkeley, an individual can make a difference, and police chief August Vollmer clearly did. In 1923, working with the Health Center, he helped establish the "bad boy clinic" and quickly won fame for his unique theory of correction. "Finis has been written to the tempestuous career of the famous old hickory stick, once the overwhelming fear of boyhood," the *Tribune* wrote beneath this headline: "Berkeley bans spanking as bad boy cure."[8]

This was, please note, eighty-four years before a state assemblywoman proposed banning spanking for kids younger than four — provoking much laughter. (Berkeley did not, however, formally ban the practice.)

Instead of the stick, the *Tribune* revealed, bad boys would face Dr. George L. Chamberlain, a university psychiatrist who adamantly opposed spanking. Chamberlain and associated doctors who volunteered their time were soon seeing fifty kids a month.

"The boy who lies and cheats, who steals and plots vengeance against his neighbors, who develops habits which alarm his parents and associates is no longer given the 'sound spanking' which was meted out to his brothers of other years," the *Tribune* said. "The cause for his maliciousness is now determined and machinery set in motion to make him a useful member of society."[9]

Berkeley's public health department continued to be city-run and innovative in later years. In 2007, for example, the *Chronicle* reported that the public health department began offering "healthy take-out" dinners prepared by local restaurants at the Frances Albrier Community Center in South Berkeley for "less than a fast food meal would cost."[10]

How Berkeley Invented Regional Parks

Berkeley dearly loved its hills but wasn't always willing to pay for them. Back in 1908, a plan to turn much of what became the Thousand Oaks neighborhood into a ninety-eight-acre wilderness park was defeated by 560 votes—even though the park was supported by everyone, from real estate developer Duncan McDuffie and the Chamber of Commerce to Benjamin Ide Wheeler and Mary McHenry Keith.[1]

Stakes were higher twenty years later when rumors circulated that the East Bay's publicly owned water company planned to sell its land along the Berkeley-Oakland hilltops to real estate speculators—land that provided the East Bay with its natural backdrop.

The property—eleven thousand acres stretching from Oakland's Chabot Reservoir in the south to Richmond in the north—had been squirreled away by a series of private water companies to ensure the cleanliness of creek water that flowed into their reservoirs. The East Bay Municipal Utility District no longer needed the acreage because it was replacing local water with purer stuff from the Mokelumne River in the Sierra.

Hill lovers quickly united to make sure that "keep out: beware of arrest" signs became a sad memory. "If we allow these properties to be subdivided and sold to private individuals," Robert Sibley, the chairman of the new East Bay Metropolitan Park Association wrote, "we will have lost forever an opportunity to build a chain of parks as beautiful as any owned by an American city today."[2]

His letter went out two weeks before Black Thursday marked the start of the Great Depression. But that put no damper on park proponents. Samuel C. May, a Cal administrator, took the lead, hiring the Olmsted brothers landscape architecture firm and Ansel Hall of the National Park Service firm to survey the potential parkland.

Founders and early leaders of the effort, who were mostly from Berkeley and Oakland, included Robert Sproul, August Vollmer, city manager Hollis Thompson, McDuffie, Major Charles Tilden, and Harold French, a pioneer conservationist with the Contra Costa Hills Club.

Through a canny campaign, largely run by Harlan Frederick, a student of Samuel May, the group convinced virtually every civic association to sign on.

But for years, despite public support, the proposed park seemed to some "a wild dream."[3] EBMUD, which still owed money to bondholders for some of its land, refused to use it for parks. "Parks are a luxury compared with a proper water supply," said George C. Pardee, the utility district's president and a former governor, "and the cheaper the water can be furnished to our people the better it will be for this community."[4]

If outdoorsmen want a park, he advised, they should create a park district and buy the land from EBMUD. Park proponents squawked, but that is what they wound up doing.

In 1933, the state passed a law that provided for such a beast as a "regional park district." In 1934, in a campaign that involved free visits to parks, parades with floats topped by children in rowboats, and federal funding for one thousand jobs for people on relief, East Bay voters agreed to create the park district: 93,405 yea, 37,397 nay.[5]

After much hashing, the new East Bay Regional Park District bought its first 2,166 acres from EBMUD—today, part of Tilden Regional Park. By the start of the twenty-first century, the district owned close to one hundred thousand acres and had its eye on thousands more.

Besides ensuring greenbelts around cities in two Bay Area counties, the park district has served as a model for urban and suburban park districts and for open space districts nationwide.

1908: *The boulders and live oaks in Thousand Oaks almost became a public park in 1908. Instead, they were surrounded with houses. Courtesy of the Bancroft Library of the University of California, Berkeley.*

1940s: *Jackie Jensen, a star fullback in the '40s for Cal coach Pappy Waldorf, relaxes with his wife, Olympic diving champ Zoe Ann Olsen, at Lake Anza in Tilden Park. Photo by Earl Rose. Courtesy of the Berkeley Historical Society, 4.8.0.195 7309.*

1950s: *The steam train at Tilden has entertained kids for generations. Photo by Earl Rose. Courtesy of the Berkeley Historical Society, 193 1176.*

1942: *Robert Gordon Sproul crowns Homecoming Queen Peggy Rich in 1942. Courtesy of the Bancroft Library of the University of California, Berkeley.*

How Berkeley's University Howled for Sproul

ultivate the art of enjoying things without owning them," Bob Sproul, who had been university president for a year, told the 1931 graduating class. "The beauty of a redwood forest, of a rushing mountain stream, of a cypress-shaded headland or a snow-carved peak is never destroyed no matter how often it may be absorbed and assimilated . . . Don't let the dead weight of material prosperity clog up the fountains of happiness."[1]

Could any sentiment be more Berkeley?

Few presidents did as much as Robert Gordon Sproul to transform the University of California from a homey, albeit superb, school into a modern juggernaut. During his tenure—1930 to 1958, the longest of any president—the university grew from 19,773 students at all its California campuses to almost that number, 19,344, at Berkeley alone. In the 1930s, the university had a medical school in San Francisco, a "Southern Branch" in Los Angeles, and an agriculture college in Davis.

By 1958, the university—which had added campuses at Riverside and Santa Barbara, and had converted the Southern Branch into the University of California, Los Angeles—was educating 47,000 students and was planning for many more.

It was Sproul who brought Ernest Lawrence to campus and supported his radiation lab, repeatedly increasing the lab's budget and staffing, and doing whatever it took to keep Lawrence. It was the lab more than anything else that caused Cal to become a scientific powerhouse in the years before and after World War II.

But none of this explains why students loved him. He was as fine a public speaker as Franklin Delano Roosevelt, Norman Thomas, or Haile Selassie, and according to one connoisseur, Sproul had "a reverberating voice and a phenomenal memory," a booming laugh, and a back-slapping manner that made him friends everywhere, from the Berkeley Rotary Club to captains of industry.[2] "At one time he belonged to 268 organizations," the *New York Times* noted.[3]

Unlike most university presidents, Sproul's background was not academe. With an undergraduate degree in civil engineering from Cal, Sproul sought work with the city of Oakland as an efficiency expert. He got the job and, efficiently enough, married the woman who interviewed him for it. Sproul rose through the university ranks in a series of comptroller jobs and still found time to help run the Save the Redwoods League and help found the Mt. Diablo Council of the Boy Scouts of America.

Like his predecessor, Benjamin Ide Wheeler, Sproul got to know many students personally, even though he lived part-time at UCLA. *Chronicle* sports reporter Will Connolly remembered running into Sproul at a university "Sirkus," "a sort of

Places

Sproul Hall, the campus's administration building, faces Sproul Plaza, a major gathering spot and longtime theater for protests and worse.

campus Mardi Gras in which the co-eds run around in little girl pinafores and the boys look silly in Buster Brown outfits." Sproul had joined the fun, almost incognito, Connolly said, "a modest guy . . . in the funny hat."[4]

In early 1939, word got out that Sproul was taking a higher-paid job at a bank—$50,000 versus his current $13,500.

All afternoon, students painted signs. They alerted Sproul's wife, Ida, who kept it to herself. By 7:30 p.m., they gathered in front of the president's mansion on campus, a Renaissance villa with a balcony above three deep arches. Sproul, Ida, and Sproul's mother stepped onto the balcony when they heard the commotion.

"More than 5,000 wildly cheering young men and women, to the accompaniment of modern tom-toms, did a tribal dance that would have made Cherokees jealous," the *Gazette* reported.

"Hey, Stay," the placards read. "We Howl for Sproul." Bands played and student body president Alan Lindsay spoke: "We have seen you around campus every day, and have spoken to you and brought our troubles to you. But until tonight we never thought it necessary to come to your house and tell you how much we like you."[5]

Sproul, his arms around his wife and his mother, announced that he had declined the bank's offer. "And this is supposed to be a commercial age," the *Gazette* editorialized. Soon everybody was singing "All Hail Blue and Gold," "even Bob's mother."[6]

Sproul, for once, was left almost speechless. "Oh boy," he told Ida, "what a swell night!"[7]

International House,

which opened in 1930, was one of the first places in Berkeley to provide integrated housing. For decades it has forged international friendships and presented multicultural events. The building is a landmark inside and out by architect George Kelham. Postcard courtesy of Sarah Wikander.

How Berkeley Cooperated

For a while, it seemed, the dream was coming true. Berkeley was forging a kinder, gentler economy, more about human needs than raw dollars.

Cal students had cooperative housing. There was the Books Unltd. Co-operative, the Arts and Crafts Co-operative, the Co-operative Center Federal Credit Union, and a Co-op Travel Agency. The Cheese Board was a co-op, and there was a cooperative bike shop. The Bay Area Funeral Society even offered a cooperative burial plan. Chief among Berkeley's co-ops was the Berkeley Co-op, which served up social activism alongside the bulk grains.

Longtime Berkeley Co-op member Fred Guy noted that people simply joined. "It's just something you do in Berkeley."[1]

The Berkeley Co-op—which at its height had three stores in Berkeley, three in Oakland and one each in El Cerrito, Castro Valley, Walnut Creek, and Marin County—was actually the second major co-op to make its mark on Berkeley. The first was the University Students' Co-operative Association, which opened in 1933, with ten men—a dozen more soon joined—sharing a small rooming house on Cal's Southside.

The inspiration was Harry Kingman, formerly an infielder with the New York Yankees, who'd been running Stiles Hall, the University's YMCA, since 1916. Kingman and his wife, Ruth, were among Berkeley's leading progressives. The Y, along with International House, was one of the few venues in town opened to Communist and other radical speakers.

To keep costs down, the student co-opers bought food in common and worked shifts around the house. Summers they toiled to earn money for the co-op, one group chopping wood in the sweltering Sacramento Valley town of Dixon. The co-op expanded, leasing fraternity houses and founding Barrington Hall, later to be infamous for rowdiness and pranks. Soon there were buildings for women, too. The co-op provided some of the first integrated student housing in Berkeley.

Many members of the students' co-op also got involved with the Berkeley Co-op, according to Bob Neptune, the first employee in its first food store and the Co-op's longtime manager.[2] The impetus for the co-op came from Berkeley's Finnish community in West Berkeley—the second largest in the United States—which had inherited the tradition from its home country. The Finns founded the Berkeley Co-operative in 1938 to run a gas station in West Berkeley.

A food store and, a few years later, a hardware store were opened in 1937 by a separate group, the Berkeley Buyers Club, which had begun a few years earlier as an Oakland-Alameda-Berkeley home-delivery by pastor Roy Wilson of the Alameda Methodist Church. Methodists played a leading role in the founding, and Neptune himself got involved through a Methodist ministry.

The cooperative gas station and grocery merged in 1947.

Lee Gomes described the idea, years later, in the *Oakland Tribune*: "Maybe, just maybe, grocery stores should exist to serve the needs of the people who shop at them, rather than simply pushing whatever marketing-driven, additive-laden food-aids a giant conglomerate happens to be trying to sell."[3]

The co-op flourished and started an associated wholesale operation. In 1947, the operations merged, forming the Consumers' Co-operative of Berkeley. More than a store, the co-op became a crusade, campaigning from its early years for

stronger consumer protection and for giving the Food and Drug Administration oversight over cosmetics.

The co-op grew rapidly, thanks to the postwar baby boom, adding stores in Berkeley and expanding to the suburbs. Innovations included home economists who talked with shoppers, taught nutrition classes, and provided recipes along with bananas and greens. The co-op pioneered unit pricing—posting by each item its per-ounce cost—and the express checkout lane. Supervised "kiddie korrals" let moms shop while their children played.

The co-op pioneered bulk bins filled with grains and whole wheat treats, had a free book exchange, and offered bulletin boards that helped people find cheap apartments, rides to Los Angeles, and wood-burning stoves. By the early 1970s, the co-op was sponsoring seed-sprouting demonstrations, followed by a "sprout-salad supper" for $1 and "natural foods feasts."[4]

It was a feel-good sort of store—usually. "When clerks smile at a corporate supermarket, it's because they know not smiling can cost them their jobs," William Brand wrote in the East Bay Express. "At the Co-op, employees have been more free to be themselves—for better or worse."[5]

From the beginning, Neptune said, the co-op was about more than selling food. The goal was to spread the word about co-ops as a different way of life. For several decades, depending on whom you ask, it worked.

"There are no product advertising displays, such as mobiles hanging from the ceiling, flashing lights or brand banners, the management feeling that such gimmicks attempt to stampede the shopper into making imprudent choices," the *Los Angeles Times* reported incredulously in the mid-1960s.[6]

Signs would even warn customers away from certain products, such as candy. "Liver is good," one note said, "but too much is not." Another: "Use regular soap, don't use deodorant soap."

Stores closed when Martin Luther King was assassinated and on Vietnam Moratorium Day. Members were proud to have low membership numbers—it meant they were longtime members. Many asked that their patron refunds be sent to the Farmworkers Union. Non-union lettuce or grapes? Not at the co-op. The co-op boycotted products from Dow Chemical to protest their manufacturing of napalm during the Vietnam War, and the store helped the Black Panthers with their free breakfast program, until what foes considered the "conservatives"—who considered themselves liberals—took control of the board.

For years the board—and co-op policies—whipsawed between socially conscious and business-is-business philosophies as the two ideologies fought it out.

By 1985, sales peaked and then declined. Labor costs were higher than the competition—and competitors had gotten better. Although it was right next door, the co-op never joined the Gourmet Ghetto. William Brand blamed "an unsuccessful transition from the age of granola to the age of radicchio."[7]

The expansion into other communities also stretched the store, though Neptune argued that growth was needed to spread increasing wages over greater sales volume.

The death was drawn out and painful, with the last two stores closing in 1988. Efforts by longtime co-opers to revive the stores failed. The *Oakland Tribune's* headline stated, "A little of Berkeley dies in death of Co-op."[8]

How Berkeley Fought World War II

Berkeley's topography wasn't radically altered by World War II, but the war did change Berkeley as profoundly as it changed any city in the country. It caused havoc in the flatlands, where many once-solid single-family homes were carved into apartments for war workers. Many of the town's residents and students died fighting. All thirteen hundred of Berkeley's Japanese were interned, losing their livelihoods in the process.

The war's biggest impact didn't become apparent until August 6, 1945, when the nuclear age opened with the bombing of Hiroshima. The atom bomb was conceived in Berkeley, and much of the early design work took place in Berkeley and at Los Alamos in New Mexico, which was directed by Berkeley physicist J. Robert Oppenheimer. The university emerged from the war as one of the world's leading scientific research institutions.

The conservative power structure that had run the city so well in so many ways before the war couldn't deal with some of the postwar changes: a black population that had quadrupled, a student population that increased 50 percent between 1941 and 1949, more cars, and a burgeoning movement for neighborhood control of neighborhoods. After the war, Berkeley would never again come across as a quiet little city.

Under a banner headline, "3,000 U.S. Casualties," *Gazette* readers learned the day after Pearl Harbor that city crews were calling off their work stoppage. "The country comes first," their leader said. "We can settle our grievances later."[1]

It was during the bombing of Pearl Harbor that a Berkeleyan made a remark that would reverberate. "Praise the Lord," the Reverend Howell Forgy told the gunnery crew, as dive bombers buzzed low, "and pass the ammunition."[2]

Four months later, the *Gazette* reported, 250 Berkeley High grads were in service—and four had died. Berkeley's first war hero emerged in June 1942, Lt. Frank T. Lobbett, who shot down a bomber off Marshall and Gilbert Islands. "Berkeleyan Bops Japanese Bomber," the *Gazette* headlined.[3] In October, twenty-two-year-old Naval Lt. William Julius Geritz won the Distinguished Service Cross for sinking a Japanese sub.

The town's favorite hero, however, was "Berkeley's ace of aces," James E. Peck, who'd learned to fly at the Oakland Airport. Turned down by the Army Air Corps because he lacked a college degree, Peck joined the Royal Air Force and won a British Distinguished Flying Cross during the terrifying Battle of Malta.

Peck and his team shot down thirty-three enemy aircraft, and he got solo credit for three kills. Later, with the U.S. Army Air Force, Peck—who was twenty-two and newly married, downed five Messerschmitts. "Combat flying is pretty grueling," he told the *Gazette*. "After about 20 or 30 minutes of such activity you are through for the day." Peck died after a crash during a training mission in 1944.[4]

Early on, Berkeleyans clearly expected another Pearl Harbor closer to home. In case of incendiary attack, people stored sand. Chemistry professor Joel Hildebrand, co-designer of a gas mask used in World War I, predicted gas attacks as well. University scientists suggested giving block wardens "2,000 wooden rattles to be used as gas signals."[5]

"It will be a miracle if the Bay Area escapes this war without at least incendiary bombs falling," columnist Hal Johnson wrote in the *Gazette*. Volunteers watched for enemy aircraft. By September 1942, Berkeley had what the War Department called "one of the five best observation posts in California," high in the hills at 708 Creston Road, thanks to Local 158 of the Carpenters Union and volunteers who manned it round the clock.[6]

1940: *Students opposed to the draft mass at Sather Gate in 1940. Sather Gate had long been used for political protests. Courtesy of the Bancroft Library of the University of California, Berkeley.*

Soon, most men remaining on campus were military and in training. The U.S. Army built a base for African American military police in town, Camp Ashby. And the U.S. Navy converted "Albany's ill-fated million dollar racetrack" at Fleming Point into a depot for landing craft, complete with a pier, hull shops, quarters for one thousand five hundred men, a one-thousand-seat theater, and a "chow hall" in the former cocktail lounge.[7]

And Berkeley turned off its lights. "Our city has long been famous for its beautiful home-covered hills and its spectacular location, lying directly opposite the Golden Gate. Now the location of our city has brought us an even greater honor, and a grave responsibility," leaders warned. "For any lights showing seaward from the higher ground in Berkeley, or creating a sky glow over our city, make easy targets of ships entering San Francisco Bay at night."[8]

Berkeley even had its own troop ship, the *Berkeley Victory*, sent into the bay on New Year's Eve 1944 while Berkeley High School's a cappella choir sang "Smooth Sailing." Berkeleyans helped equip the ship with movies and books, and more than ten thousand turned out for "the biggest and most colorful launching ever experienced in the Bay Area."[9]

Cooperation was less forthcoming for federal efforts to provide war worker housing. While barrack-like dwellings—and, occasionally, well-designed but simple modern housing—quickly went up in Richmond and Vallejo, Berkeley's city council consistently opposed plans to build "temporary tenement" dwellings.[10]

The city did relax building codes and allowed homes to be subdivided, and much housing was provided on and around the campus. A few dozen Cape Cod–style bungalows plus several hundred apartments were built by private developers in West Berkeley for war workers. A temporary commuter railroad ran through Berkeley to the Richmond shipyards.

Many war workers flooding the Bay Area were blacks from the South, and opposition to housing them was tinged with

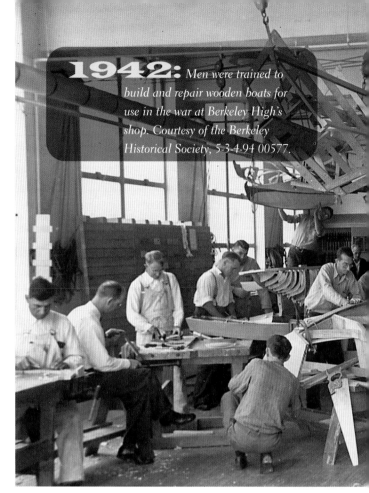

1942: *Men were trained to build and repair wooden boats for use in the war at Berkeley High's shop. Courtesy of the Berkeley Historical Society, 5-3-4-94 00577.*

racism. "It will undoubtedly draw into the community the type of resident which is going to be a burden immediately upon the cessation of hostilities," one property owner complained about plans for war housing in the city's industrial zone.[11]

The city fought federal efforts to build temporary war housing at the border with Albany. More than four hundred and fifty units in Berkeley and close to eight hundred in Albany made up Codornices Village, which wound up less than temporary. Codornices Village was later converted to university family student housing.

How Berkeley's Japanese Persevered through Adversity

When Bess Yasukochi, a secretary in Berkeley's public health department, heard that Pearl Harbor had been bombed she felt "disbelief and shock. I broke down and cried."[1] Berkeley's 1,300 Japanese residents, some of whom had been in town for generations, anticipated the worst—and got it.

Like Japanese Americans up and down the coast, Berkeley's Japanese were ordered to prepare for internment as the authorities worried about potential espionage and sabotage, and Roosevelt signed Executive Order 9066.

Internees could bring with them belongings weighing up to three hundred pounds—but no pets. Families were split apart, sometimes for good. People lost their professions and businesses. Many lost their homes. The fear was intense. Some people were convinced they would be killed or forced into slave labor.

Hours after the attack on Pearl Harbor, the FBI came for the father of Yushiko Uchida, who described the experience in *Desert Exile: The Uprooting of a Japanese-American Family.* Posters warned Japanese to stay home after 8 p.m. Kurasaburo and Kikuyu Fujii had to shutter their University Laundry—losing their investment of a lifetime. They got a neighbor to watch over their house, which was rented out while they were interned.

The Uchida's last breakfast at home was as cheerful as they could make it, shared with Caucasian neighbors who drove them to the debarkation at First Congregational Church. When Yushiko Uchida, who was a senior at Cal, saw the guards, she said, "My knees sagged, my stomach began to churn and I almost lost my breakfast."[2]

The soldiers who herded them out of town said the evacuation was for their own good, Yasukochi remembered. "If they were protecting us," she asked, "why were their guns pointed at us?"[3]

Haruko Obata, the son of artist and professor Chiura Obata, reported: "The soldiers were polite to Papa because his papers said that he was a university professor. They were respectful and felt badly for us and one said he was very sorry in a low voice."[4]

Japanese were bussed first to Tanforan Race Track on the Peninsula, where accommodations were filthy and cold. "We were herded into a horse pen," Min Sano, who was a young girl, recalled.[5] Within weeks they were taken to camps in the deserts of Central California or Utah.

It's remarkable how clear-headed many remained as they tried to retain normalcy in lives that were being torn apart. Young Frank Kawahara, while detained in Tanforan, worried because he hadn't returned a book to the Berkeley Library. "We had such a short notice to evacuate that we 'jammed' all unnecessary articles in a friend's basement," he wrote the librarian. "I wish, Miss Smith, that you would inform me of the cost of the book. I will try to pay for its cost."

Miss Smith told him to forget it "since it is not exactly your fault," and instead sent boxes of books to Tanforan.[6]

1943: *George and Michiko Uchida, the daughter of Kurasaburo and Kikuyu Fujii, didn't let the approaching internment stop them. They married two days before being taken to Tanforan. Photo by Dorothea Lange. Courtesy of the Bancroft Library of the University of California, Berkeley.*

And, while people in many cities jeered as their Japanese neighbors were rounded up in parking lots, Berkeleyans eased the strain. The city's Japanese "were the beneficiaries of a quiet protest unheard of elsewhere in those dark days after the Japanese attack on Pearl Harbor," wrote Robert Yamada, a researcher with the Berkeley Historical Society.[7]

Throughout town, hostesses from churches served sandwiches and tea. Church members helped find places for people to store belongings and to house their pets.

Even Japanese-Americans who joined the service could be locked up. John Naoki Fujii, whose parents owned Berkeley's University Laundry, enlisted in the Army Air Corps the day after Pearl Harbor—only to find himself in a guarded stockade

Berkeley did what it could. Many Berkeleyans tried to fend off Executive Order 9066, including university president Robert Sproul, Mayor Frank Gaines, and ex-police chief Vollmer. Through the Fair Play Committee, International House director Allen Blaisdell; Harry and Ruth Kingman, who ran the YMCA's Stiles Hall; photographer Dorothea Lange and her husband, economist Paul Taylor; and others fought internment and helped its victims.

for the first month along with other Japanese recruits.[8]

When the Fujii family returned to Berkeley after the war, Naoki's father, Kurasaburo, who'd been forced to sell the successful family laundry at a huge loss, ended up working two part-time jobs as a custodian and a janitor for the rest of his working life.

1942:
Chiura Obata, one of the Bay Area's best artists and a professor at Cal, kept a visual diary during his internment at Topaz, Utah. This painting shows the debarkation from Berkeley.

april 30 1942
First Congregational
Church, Berkeley

How Berkeley Invented the Bomb

rtistically, UC Berkeley can be seen as a self-satisfied suburb of a provincial city. Science, though, is another story. The university is a leading research institution, and it all started with the bomb.

More precisely, it started with Ernest O. Lawrence, the physicist whose development of the cyclotron—the "atom smasher"—at Berkeley attracted more physicists and, ultimately, gave Berkeley the lead research role in the development of the atom bomb during World War II. It was Lawrence who brought Berkeley its first Nobel Prize in 1939 for the cyclotron.

Though peace-loving Berkeleyans may hate to admit it, the atom bomb was largely conceived in Berkeley by scientists associated with Cal, although the hands-on work—producing U-235 and plutonium, assembling components,

testing—took place elsewhere. The plutonium powering the bomb that exploded over Nagasaki was discovered at Berkeley.

J. Robert Oppenheimer, the Berkeley physicist, led the project's research team and directed the Los Alamos lab. The top-secret effort, in fact, spanned the country, with research underway in Chicago, New York, and many other cities and universities. Scientists came from all over, including Europe.

The Wet Suit

ot every scientific advance in Berkeley won a Nobel Prize. One that did not, but is notable nonetheless, was the invention of the wet suit by Hugh Bradner in the early 1950s. Divers and surfers have been thanking him ever since.

The suit's development shows just how scientifically important and versatile an institution Cal had become. Bradner, a Cal physicist at the radiation laboratory, had the inspiration that underwater swimmers could stay warm without staying dry—hence, the term "wet" suit. Air bubbles trapped in the material would provide warmth.

The effort, which was originally undertaken for the U.S. Marine Corps and the U.S. Navy, involved a team of scientists and engineers from the university.

A prototype designed for commercial use was produced in 1952. Bradner never patented the suit and never tried to profit from it. His interest remained scientific; he went on to serve as a professor at the Scripps Institute of Oceanography at UC San Diego.

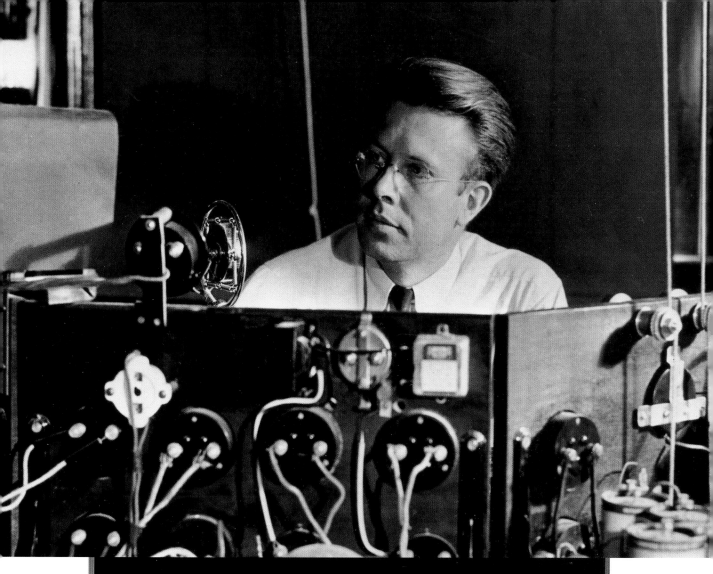

1938: *Ernest Lawrence in his radiation lab, at the controls of the thirty-seven-inch cyclotron in 1938. Courtesy of the Bancroft Library of the University of California, Berkeley.*

Headquarters was briefly in New York City, hence the name "Manhattan Project."

"Lawrence was the spark that turned the University of California from a backwater institution to a world leader in science," said Charles Shank, who was later head of the Lawrence Berkeley Laboratory.[1]

Lawrence, Berkeley's youngest professor when he was hired at age twenty-seven in 1928, created the Radiation Lab with president Sproul's strong backing. The lab developed the cyclotron—at first a four-inch device but by the end of the war, 184 inches—that used magnets to speed up and eventually smash atomic particles. Besides inventing nuclear medicine, the lab helped make the bomb possible.

For a time, Lawrence and "Oppie," as he was called, were close friends, spinning out theories while walking in the Berkeley Hills or listening to classical albums at Oppie's home in the hills. Physicists hashed out details of the atomic bomb over dinners at Spenger's and Trader Vic's. It was at Spenger's that Edward Teller discussed his idea for a "Super-bomb"—later called the H-bomb—and warned that its explosion might set off a chain reaction that would incinerate the planet.

The paradox—Bohemian, Leftie, and seat-of-the-pants Berkeley helping develop an atom bomb in top-secret—was apparent early on, especially to such federal overseers as the FBI. From early 1941, shortly after Lawrence embarked on a crash program to develop the bomb, Washington worried about his "cavalier attitude to security," according to historian Gregg Herken, whose eye-opening "Brotherhood of the Bomb" draws from declassified U.S. government files, Soviet communications with American spies, and Communist Party records.[2]

The feds had reason to worry about Lawrence's lackadaisical security. A federal investigator simply walked up "Cyclotron Hill" above campus and spent hours perusing "secret" blueprints unmolested.

ON LABORATORY, UNIVERSITY OF CALIFORNIA, BERKELEY, CALIFORNIA   210

9B-H666

But it was Oppenheimer who really had federal officials quaking because of his friendships with Communists and other leftists, including his wife and his brother, and his involvement with Communist front organizations. Oppenheimer was also suspected of treason because he refused to divulge the name of a friend who'd been contacted by a Soviet spy. The spy wanted to meet scientists who were working on the bomb. Oppenheimer did tell investigators about the incident, however, and under pressure finally revealed the name of his friend, Haakon Chevalier.

Oppenheimer's phone and home were bugged, and he was assigned two "bodyguards" whose job was to spy on him. Army counterintelligence agents worked from a spy house south of campus. When Oppie and Chevalier conversed at Oppie's home in the hills, they did so in a wooded grove to avoid detection. The FBI set up a project dubbed CINRAD (Communist Infiltration of the Radiation Laboratory).

Oppenheimer was finally stripped of his security clearance in 1954, in part because he opposed developing an H-bomb—the issue that destroyed his friendship with Lawrence.

Although Oppenheimer never betrayed the United States, some of his Manhattan Project colleagues had done so, including young scientists who were seen giving documents to Soviet agents. Several were fired. One was drafted, to get him out of the way while keeping the story quiet. Later he was unsuccessfully prosecuted.

Scientists and policy makers agonized about the decision to use the bomb. Lawrence "was the last to come around on actually bombing Hiroshima," his wife, Mary, claimed, years later.[3] The day after the bomb dropped on Hiroshima and the day before it fell on Nagasaki, the Berkeley *Gazette* bragged: "Credit UC prof for new bomb," meaning Oppenheimer. Three weeks later, the paper proclaimed, "UC helped to end war, ensure peace."[4] Berkeley scientists, led by Edward Teller, were already developing the H-bomb.

The University's Nobelists

The Nobels have kept coming for Cal scientists, social scientists, and humanists. A recent count listed twenty Cal faculty and twenty-four alumni winners.

Chemists John Northrop and Wendell Stanley won for preparation of pure forms of enzymes and virus proteins in 1946, and chemist William Giauque won for a magnetic refrigeration system in 1949. In 1951, Edwin McMillan won for discovering neptunium, and Glenn Seaborg for plutonium; two years later Owen Chamberlain and Emilio Segré won for discovering the anti-proton.

Donald Glaser won the prize in 1960 for developing the bubble chamber, a useful tool in the study of atomic physics. Luis Alvarez won the prize eight years later for improving on the bubble chamber.

In 1997, Steven Chu won the prize for using lasers to "trap" atoms in place for easier study.

Winners in economics have included Gerard Debreu (1983), John Harsanyi (1994), and George Akerloff (2001), who explained why markets do not always behave as economists predict.

Poet Czeslaw Milosz won the Nobel Prize in literature in 1980.

How Berkeley Challenged the Establishment

How Berkeley Invented
Listener-Sponsored Radio

Fifteen months after KPFA debuted as the world's first listener-sponsored radio station, it went dead—as per plan, its founder claimed. Lew Hill started the station as an experiment. Give listeners high-quality radio—then take it away—and then ask them to pony up to get it back.

Starting in April 1949, the low-powered station that didn't reach much beyond Berkeley had featured plays by Shakespeare, Chekhov, Euripides, Shaw, and Ibsen, "sometimes lasting more than three hours without interruption," according to the *Chronicle*'s Bernard Taper. There were readings of Verlaine, Baudelaire, and Rilke, often in the original language. Allen Ginsberg read "Howl" over the air, infuriating censors who tried to ban the poem.[1]

Thirty-eight classical works, many by local composers, had their radio premieres. Listeners heard commentary by Democrats, Republicans, Socialists, anarchists, pacificists—but no Communists, "because we have never been able to find a Communist willing to speak as a human rather than as a party machine," Hill said.

"This small station was a heretic from the huckster's orthodoxy of radio operation—in the way it tried to finance itself, in the high intellectual level of its programs and, in fact, in its whole atmosphere," Taper wrote, adding, "It went on the unusual assumption that its listeners were not dopes."[1]

Composer George Barati was soon chairing public meetings in support. "We intend to put it back on the air in a few months," he said, "and this time we are going to keep it on the air." KPFA returned to the air in May 1951—with enough power to reach from San Jose to Santa Rosa. Subscribers paid $10 a year.

Although there had been public radio stations from radio's birth in the 1920s, many college run, by the 1940s most were gone. And listener sponsorship, though proposed in the past, had never taken hold.

KPFA's success won international attention. The Ford Foundation contributed $150,000 and proclaimed KPFA a model for other stations. KPFA opened its first sister station, KPFK, in Los Angeles in 1964.

For decades, KPFA featured New Music when composer-promoter Charles Amirkhanian was music director. In the '70s, a KPFA bus traveled the town, encouraging participation: "Foghorns, tympani, license plates, gongs, saxophones, guitars and garbage cans are all welcome. Anything that sounds is fair game. Do something strange!"[2] Johnny Otis and Phil Elwood played rhythm and blues, jazz, La Onda Bajita, Hispanic soul, and

1970s: *Composer and vocalist Meredith Monk visits Charles Amirkhanian, a composer and KPFA's music director, at the stations's studio. Courtesy of Charles Amirkhanian.*

doo-wop. Phil Lesh, then a station volunteer, introduced Jerry Garcia to the wider world on the show *The Midnight Special*.

Over the years, talk shows have veered from intellectually challenging to intellectually challenged, featuring music from Bach to political hip-hop. Bluesman Homesick James and conceptual artist Tom Marioni were volunteers. Robert Creeley hosted a festival of underground poetry. "The Unspeakable Doctor Schrog" read "tales of eldritch terror." *Anarchy Today* was a popular show at the start of the 1970s, as was a show explaining how the CIA toppled the Twin Towers in the 2000s.

Sometimes it proved too much. The financial news journal *Barrons* took exception when Pacifica, KPFA's parent, sought a Washington, D.C., station in 1970. "Air Wave Pollution," the headline sputtered, "the Pacifica Foundation has broadcast it for years."[3]

"Programs broadcast recently over wholly-owned Pacifica stations have featured regular news commentaries by identified Communists and Black Panthers, made by Radio Hanoi, Red Chinese propaganda and advocacy of blowing up police stations and fire houses." "All Pacifica stations . . . readily acknowledge that they regularly broadcast programs by homosexuals for homosexuals."[4]

The Senate and the Federal Communications Commission investigated, and it looked like the entire network might be closed. But in the end, Pacifica got the new station.

While KPFA has never prospered in the usual sense of the term, it never lost its hold on its listeners—despite an almost unending series of crises.

One of the earliest crises involved Hill, who came from a wealthy family and was a disappointed poet, a Pacifist, and a Quaker. Though he attended a military prep school, he was a conscientious objector during World War II.

Two years after KPFA had returned to the air, Hill was battling the station board over whose word carried most weight. He quit as chairman and then returned. In 1957, the board overruled Hill after several firings. On July 30, depressed and in constant pain from an incurable back condition, he ended his life at his cabin on the Russian River by running the exhaust pipe into his car. He'd attempted suicide several times before, his wife said. His note: "Not from anger or despair but for peace."[5]

Any station that has had a paid bureaucracy, paid and volunteer programmers that represent a wide range of interests, a listeners' board, a Third World Bureau, and a parent organization is bound to see conflict. KPFA has had strikes, accusations of mismanagement and incompetence, even spurts of dead air. The station was off the air for a month in 1974 when the manager tried to fire a third of the staff, including all its African Americans.

In 1999, the parent Pacifica network locked KPFA's employees out of the station—actually yanking one off the air in a dispute about local control and freedom of the airwaves. Fans were afraid Pacifica would sell the station. Hundreds were arrested in protests outside the station, and more than ten thousand attended one rally. Pacifica finally relented. Among the signs displayed by KPFA fans outside the station was "Honk for free speech." As the *New York Times* reported, "Everybody did."[6]

How Berkeley Swore an Oath

It was a frightened time. Red China had emerged as a Communist menace. By the end of the year the Soviets would test their first atomic bomb. In Sacramento, legislative committees were pounding on the university. Senator Jack Tenney held hearings from 1946 through 1948 accusing professors and students alike of treason.

In January 1949, the university's comptroller suggested a ploy to fend off state legislators. Have our employees vow, "I am not a member of the Communist Party, or under any oath, or a party to any agreement, or under any commitment that is in conflict with my obligation under this oath." President Robert Gordon Sproul approved. So did the Regents. Not so the employees, who saw the move as a way to destroy the system of

1950s: *Faculty, students, and staff filled the Greek Theatre to protest the oath. Courtesy of the Bancroft Library of the University of California, Berkeley.*

tenure and stifle academic freedom. Mass protests were held at the Greek Theatre.

"That was an insult, an absolute insult," said Robert Royston, the landscape architect, who quit rather than take the oath. "I felt very strongly about it because I had been taking loyalty oaths all the time while I was in the Navy."[1]

Across the country, anti-Communist hysteria convinced the federal government, other public agencies, and some businesses to insist that their employees sign loyalty oaths. But nowhere was the resistance so intense—or the nationwide attention so great—as at the University of California in Berkeley. The battle against the oath galvanized resistance elsewhere and inspired proponents of free speech for decades to come.

"Men and women of spirit object to having a knife put at their throats," said George R. Stewart, a Berkeley English professor and writer who wrote *The Year of the Oath*.[2]

In 1950, thirty-one members of the faculty lost their jobs in "the August expulsions." Dozens of other staff members and teaching assistants were fired. Others quit in protest. Much research was suspended, and morale bottomed out as people stared at "the vacant desks of our colleagues."[3]

The battle went on for three years. Sproul eventually argued against the oath—but the regents insisted. This would be the first of several occasions, including the Free Speech Movement and People's Park, when efforts on the part of UC administrators to head off confrontations were scotched by the regents.

World events added to the din. In June 1950, North Korean troops poured across the border into South Korea. The draft was reinstated and several members of the faculty were called up. That same year, United States Senator Joe McCarthy charged that the State Department was riddled with Communists. It also came out in blazing headlines that the Russians owed their new atomic bomb to spies and Communist sympathizers, including some who had infiltrated Berkeley's Radiation Lab during the war.

"State Report accuses UC as aiding Reds," one headline read, followed by, "Say campus spy hotbed during war." Sproul was accused of aiding the Communist conspiracy by allowing Reds to infiltrate the university.[4]

Many of the fired faculty were rehired in 1952 (and eventually given back pay) after the state Supreme Court ruled that the law had unconstitutionally singled out only one class of state employee. The United States Supreme Court ruled loyalty oaths unconstitutional in 1967. But the university had suffered deeply. Friendships were destroyed, careers blighted, studies disrupted, and distrust of the university heightened. The tragedy would have repercussions in the 1960s.

How Berkeley Broke the Racial Barrier

By all accounts, D. G. Gibson was a quiet man—silent at times. Slow-talking and slow-moving, he could appear to be asleep. But watch out.

"The listening—I can't emphasize it enough—the act of listening, was his way of providing for the political participation of everyone," said Evillio Grillo, a disciple. "Listening was his method. If you don't understand that, you'd miss the whole point. You'd see him as a boss rather than what he was: a leader."[1]

A Berkeley resident since the mid-1920s, when there were only five hundred blacks in town, Gibson distributed black newspapers and cosmetics from a shop on Sacramento Street. Although they lived in a de facto ghetto, Berkeley's blacks built a healthy community with their own stores, communal organizations, and churches.

1939: *By 1939, the neighborhood around Ashby Avenue and Sacramento Street had become a thriving black commercial strip. Photographer John Eskridge. Courtesy of the Berkeley Historical Society, 415-193-2234.*

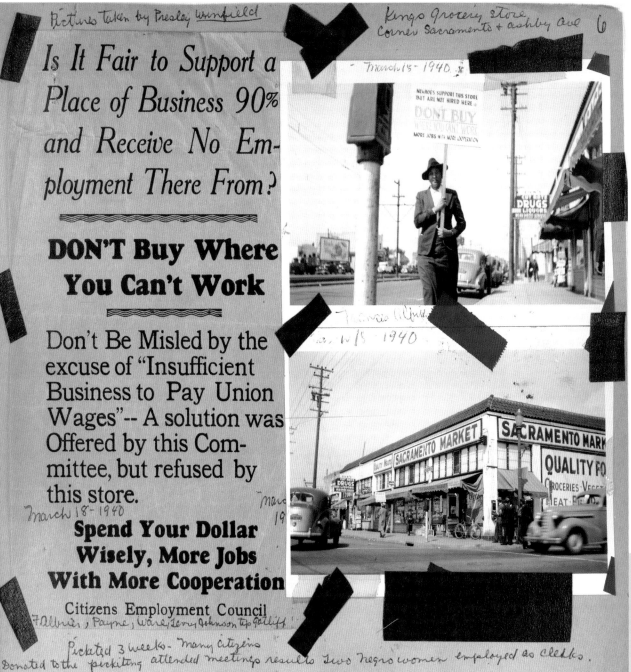

Pictures taken by Presley Winfield

Kings Grocery Store Corner Sacramento & Ashby Ave 6

Is It Fair to Support a Place of Business 90% and Receive No Employment There From?

DON'T Buy Where You Can't Work

Don't Be Misled by the excuse of "Insufficient Business to Pay Union Wages"-- A solution was Offered by this Committee, but refused by this store.

Spend Your Dollar Wisely, More Jobs With More Cooperation

Citizens Employment Council

March 15 - 1940.

NEGROES SUPPORT THIS STORE BUT ARE NOT HIRED HERE
DON'T BUY WHERE YOU CAN'T WORK
MORE JOBS WITH MORE COOPERATION

March 15 - 1940

SACRAMENTO MARKET
QUALITY FOODS
GROCERIES · VEGET
MEAT

March 18 - 1940

Picketed 3 weeks - many citizens Donated to the picketing attended meetings results Two Negro women employed as clerks.

144

Leon Frederic March, Berkeley's first black letter carrier (1905) and his wife, Vivian, organized a free childcare center in South Berkeley. Around the same time, 1918, Walter Gordon was doing well as a student at Cal, captaining the football team. "How's that for democracy!" co-ed Agnes Edwards crowed.[2] He got his doctorate in law from Boalt Hall while working days as Berkeley's first black cop. Gordon later became a prominent attorney, governor of the Virgin Islands, and a federal judge.

But almost no African Americans worked downtown or for the university. Signs proclaimed "No Negro trade solicited" in front of many stores. When Gibson and Sacramento Street pharmacist William Byron Rumford complained to the police in the mid-1930s about the signs, they were told, "no law against it." Rumford, a former boxer ("Fighting Joe Gans") with a pleasant manner, said, "Well, we could remove those signs ourselves."[3] The signs were soon gone.

c. 1950s: *William Byron Rumford. Courtesy of the Bancroft Library of the University of California, Berkeley.*

Berkeley's business-oriented, Republican white leaders didn't know it, but their days were numbered. Berkeley's black population was 3,400 in 1940 (4 percent of the population) and jumped to 13,289 by 1950 (almost 12 percent of the population), thanks to World War II defense jobs that attracted emigrants from the South. Black population in Berkeley peaked in 1970 at 27,400 (23.5 percent of the population).

But numbers don't automatically translate into power. Through their East Bay Political Club, Gibson and Rumford devised strategies and groomed candidates. According to journalist Bill Wyman, Gibson's system was, "Volunteer, get involved, and learn to understand the system; run for office but don't run against each other and split your support; register your supporters and get out the vote."[4]

The first black person to run for city council was Frances Albrier, "a fearless young woman from Tuskegee, Alabama, who was not afraid to challenge the establishment," according to Ruth Acty, Berkeley's first black public school teacher; she owed her job to Albrier, who came in ninth in the 1939 race.[5] Lawyer Tom Berkeley did better in 1947, coming up three hundred votes short.

The next year, Gibson convinced Rumford to run for state assembly. He won—but only after going to court to demand a recount.

Rumford, the first African American elected to statewide office in Northern California, authored two antidiscrimination laws, the Fair Employment Practices Act of 1959, and the Fair Housing ("Rumford") Act of 1963.

The fight against housing discrimination was one of the most convulsive in Berkeley's history. The newly liberal city council passed a city ordinance banning housing discrimination in 1961—but it was tossed out by the voters in '62 during a referendum campaign that was tinged with racism, with some realtors vowing never to sell Berkeley Hills homes to blacks. The vote was 22,750 to repeal fair housing, 20,456 to keep it.

Meanwhile, the state legislature approved the Rumford Fair Housing Act, essentially making Berkeley's repeal of its own housing ordinance moot (though Berkeley's law had been stronger). But the Rumford Act itself was invalidated by voters a year after it passed in a campaign funded by realtors. The measure that repealed the act also barred the state from any further actions to ban housing discrimination.

Ironically, perhaps, this time Berkeley voted not to repeal the act but to support fair housing—one sign that the city was moving toward the left. In any case, both the state and United States Supreme Courts later ruled the measure that repealed fair housing unconstitutional. The Rumford Act was law again.

Rumford was a father figure in South Berkeley, making the rounds of cafes and barbershops, and holding court. "If you came to him with a problem," Viola Taylor Wims said, "he could say five words and solve it."[6]

In 1961, Berkeley finally elected its first African American to the city council, Wilmont Sweeney, "a big man with a strong handshake and an easy, affable manner."[7] The liberal slate that helped elect Sweeney also gave Berkeley its first African American on the school board, Reverend Roy Nichols. Sweeney served on the council until 1964, when he was named a superior court judge.

Berkeley's first black mayor, Warren Widener—a "radical"—was elected in 1971, beating Sweeney—a "liberal"—by forty-nine votes. Gibson's "don't run against each other" rule was out of date.

By this time, liberal Berkeley was turning radical, as the Vietnam War galvanized the left. Ron Dellums, briefly a radical city councilman and then Berkeley's first black representative in Congress, flew in for Widener's inauguration, which the *Gazette* called "a swinging, contemporary inaugural ceremony." It featured folk, rock, and gospel bands. "Fashions included floor-length, street-length, and hot pants under long skirts slit to the waistline." Reverend Cecil William's invocation ended, "Jesus Christ. Right on!"[8] Days later, Widener told the Rotary Club, "I can work with you."[9]

Widener was soon regarded as a turncoat by his radical supporters for dropping his support of rent control and community control of the police. He also changed his mind about paying city employees for forty hours a week while working only thirty. Loni Hancock, then a radical councilwoman and later an assemblywoman and mayor, dubbed him, "The Lyndon Johnson of Berkeley."[10]

In 1979, Widener, who first beat Sweeney by coming from his left, lost his third bid for mayor to a black man who ran to Widener's left—Gus Newport, Berkeley's second socialist mayor, and its first socialist mayor in sixty-six years.

Places

South Berkeley has an affordable public housing project, the William Byron Rumford Senior Plaza on Sacramento Street, and the Frances Albrier Community Center at San Pablo Park.

How Berkeley Pioneered School Integration

In 1962, all eyes were on the fight to integrate the University of Mississippi. In April 1968, they peered at Berkeley. *Time* magazine and the *New York Times* were there, as were state and federal officials.

"We have the chance to make school history here or to destroy that chance," Berkeley's superintendent of schools, Neil Sullivan, announced, as twenty-six buses began hauling three thousand five hundred of the district's nine thousand elementary school children from one side of town to the next, uphill and down. "Can integration survive here and in the nation? What is done here will determine the future of integration."[1]

Berkeley had become the first city in the nation with more than one hundred thousand residents, and a good-sized population of African Americans, to desegregate its schools voluntarily—without court order. It put Berkeley on the map. The school population was 50 percent white, 41 percent black, and the rest mostly Asian and Hispanic.

As it turned out, 1968 was anticlimactic. The federal Office of Civil Rights found no problems whatsoever—other than what Robert Coles called "those nods, grimaces, stares which even teachers sometimes missed."[2] "Things are going mighty well," the school district's assistant superintendent reported a few weeks later.[3]

But integration didn't happen without a fight or without white flight. Things went well in 1968 because the process had begun a decade earlier. That's when the city was shocked. By the late 1960s, the fighting was over. Berkeley had been transformed.

The effort to integrate schools started in 1957 with Reverend Roy Nichols, then head of the local NAACP. In '58, Berkeley students were 63.3 percent white, 28.7 percent black, 7.9 percent "other" (mostly "Oriental").

Although schools were never officially segregated by race, many were either mostly black or mostly white because they were neighborhood schools, and few blacks lived in the hills. According to 1963 figures, most hillside elementary schools were 95 percent white, some flatland schools 90 percent black. In the black schools, students averaged a year behind grade level. In the white schools, they were a year ahead.

"Although the majority of Caucasians in Berkeley in their outward behavior exhibit no prejudices toward the Negro race," a committee reported, "there is no question but that a great deal of latent prejudice exists among the people of our community."[4]

When Judge Redmond Staats, a proponent of integration, announced at a public meeting a year later that "Berkeley, considering its size, probably has the highest Negro population of any city north of the Mason-Dixon line," the *Gazette* reported, "a murmur of astonishment went up from the audience."[5]

Over the next decade, murmurs would give way to shouting as one committee after another—the Staats Committee, the Hadsell Committee—prepared plans and as the schools carried them out. By 1960, starting out slowly, the schools were assigning teachers to schools without regard to race. Things speeded up once the school board became dominated by liberals in 1961 with the election of Roy Nichols and Carol Sibley.

By 1963, the schools had boosted their minority hiring—going from forty-five black employees in 1959 to seventy-six, and from twenty-one Asians to thirty-two.

And the board agreed to integrate the schools, redrawing boundaries so black kids from the flatlands would attend white schools in the hills and vice versa. The plan was to integrate the junior high schools first, in part by reconfiguring grade structure. The elementary schools would be integrated later. Integration for junior high students happened in 1964. Since Berkeley had only one high school, it had always been integrated.

Critics, calling the junior high integration of 1964 "integration at the point of a pistol," mounted a recall.[6] Along with the referendum a year earlier that killed fair housing in Berkeley, the school recall was one of the defining moments in the town's political history. That the recall failed by a two-thirds margin indicated to contemporary observers that Berkeley was indeed becoming liberal.

Recall leaders never focused on race. They called the integration plan a "radical" attempt to end neighborhood schooling that would harm the town's high-achieving junior highs. But the furor the integration plan aroused suggested deeper motives among some recall backers.

Sibley—whose late husband, Robert, had spearheaded the movement to create the East Bay Regional parks—got crank calls every hour of the day and night and was called a Communist. The president of her church refused to speak to her. "But once the recall was over and we got going again, there didn't seem to be a lasting ugliness. I don't know whether it was because a lot of people moved out of town or what," she told an oral historian, with a wry laugh.[7]

In fact, foes of integration had predicted white flight from the start. "Berkeley will become an all-Negro community," one resident warned in 1964.[8] And although it's hard to quantify, many Berkeleyans did leave town for Orinda, Lafayette, and other suburban towns, radically reshaping the town's political and social life. Perhaps nothing made Berkeley more Berkeley than population shifts that followed integration in the 1960s.

"The student racial census" of 1967 found no sign of a "mass exodus of Caucasians from the School System in order to avoid integration."[9] In fact, the proportion of white and black students remained stable through the late 1960s and early 1970s. Still, what was happening was clear to many observers, including researchers from the United States Commission on Civil

1966: *An all-black class at Columbus School in 1966, the year before busing came to Berkeley's elementary schools. Courtesy of the Berkeley Historical Society.*

WHITTIER SCHOOL
1776   1976
MRS CHRISTESON
MRS PRICE
GRADES KDGN & 1

Rights: "When whites left the district, they were replaced by other white families who wanted to move into the district."[10]

By mid-1967, the school board decided that elementary school busing was needed to complete the work that had been started in '64. "Some residents will just plain not accept busing and will move," the *Gazette* said.[11] The board adopted the plan unanimously at the start of 1968—the year Martin Luther King and Robert Kennedy were assassinated and riots broke out in cities across the country.

Superintendent Sullivan attributed integration's success to careful planning and community involvement. "This was brought about by the largest master plan committee in the world, I guess. It had at least two hundred active people with several thousand others involved. That was the beginning of the community movement in Berkeley."[12]

By 1968, though, the conversation about race had gone beyond integration. Now people wanted self-determination and black power. Weeks after complete integration was achieved, Ron Stevenson of the high school's Black Students

Union stood before the school board and demanded a black curriculum, "five black counselors and we want them in two to four weeks," "three black cooks and soul food cooked three times a week," and African dance added to physical education. Tracking students by performance should be ended, and "all racist teachers and administrators be removed from the school."[13]

The board didn't bother to appoint a committee. They unanimously announced "general support."

lier by banning student groups from haranguing each other about noncampus issues while on campus.

None of this, by the way, is what brought Weinberg his greatest fame. That came when he advised his peers, "Never trust anyone over 30."[2]

It had all begun two weeks earlier, when campus officials ordered student activists to remove their tables from Sather Gate just before school reopened in 1964, while Kerr was out of town.

Bad timing. Student activism was already high, thanks to

How Berkeley Promoted Free Speech

Ilona Hancock—she was called Loni when she became Berkeley's mayor twenty-two years later—was innocently wheeling her baby across campus on October 1, 1964, when she came upon a disturbing scene. A police car was parked in front of the administration building, Sproul Hall, guarded by police officers, surrounded by two thousand chanting students, with Mario Savio on top of the car making speeches and a single student inside—Jack Weinberg—smoking a cigarette, biding his time.[1]

He had lots of time to bide. Weinberg remained in the car, captive of police and of history, for thirty-two hours—let out occasionally to pee and to speak to supporters. Soon, Savio and other leaders of the Free Speech Movement engaged in sweaty negotiations with Cal president Clark Kerr and the ham-fisted subordinates who had instigated the crisis two months ear-

1964: *Jack Weinberg—inside the police car as the Free Speech Movement started all around him. Courtesy of the Bancroft Library of the University of California, Berkeley.*

President Kennedy's call for community volunteers. Students were returning to Cal after summering with the Peace Corps. Others had registered black voters in the South or worked with the Freedom Riders during Mississippi's Freedom Summer. Johnson was running a scare campaign in his race against Goldwater for president, showing TV spots of a mushroom cloud to suggest the world's future under a Republican president. The Republican convention had just finished up across the bay in San Francisco.

And, historically, the area outside Sather Gate had always been off campus, and thus okay for student speech about off-campus issues. The construction of the Student Union and Sproul Plaza incorporated this area into the campus proper in the late 1950s, but it had remained traditional to hold political events there.

On September 30, the day before Weinberg's arrest, five hundred students occupied Sproul Hall in protest. They came with guitars, sleeping bags, and "enough food to last an army a week." Folk songs resounded. Free speech attracted students of all political persuasions. "Outside, on the steps of Sproul hall," the *Examiner* reported, "white-shirted Goldwater supporters sang and shouted in support of those locked inside."

"Police, plainly anxious to go home themselves, wandered from one group to the next asking, 'Don't you want to go home?'"[3]

What began that night culminated in early December in the largest demonstration any university in America had ever seen and the largest mass arrests in the state's history, about eight hundred protesters.

The Free Speech Movement, which rocked Berkeley and the nation in 1964, proved historically important—inspiring people worldwide to speak out, to get involved, to block nuclear plants in Bodega Bay, and to stop urban renewal demolitions in Oakland. After the Free Speech Movement, politicians knew what citizen participation meant. Governing the people would never be the same.

By the mid-1960s, Cal no longer seemed the friendly tree-shaded place where students chatted with avuncular president Wheeler while he clomped through on his horse.

It was part of the military industrial complex and a "multiversity" in the making, to use Kerr's term. Kerr, Berkeley's chancellor from 1952 to 1958, wanted a statewide university that could educate all Californians—which meant it had to be big. From 1958 to 1967, university enrollment doubled systemwide, from 45,303 students to 87,000.

Although Kerr, a liberal Democrat, repeatedly tried to meet student demands, efforts to punish the Free Speech Movement's leaders kept the battle going, as did the occasional faux pas, such as campus police manhandling Savio when he took to the stage at a Greek Theatre rally called to cool off rising tensions between students and administrators. It also didn't help that the University Regents consistently opposed liberalizing campus policy on political activity.

Also energizing the Free Speech Movement was the fact that its leaders were fine speakers and show people. Savio "spoke to a generation," the *Chronicle* later observed.[4]

"There is a time," Savio intoned, "when the operation of the machine becomes so odious, makes you sick at heart, that you can't take part. You can't even tacitly take part. And you've got to put your bodies upon the gears and upon the wheels, upon the levers, upon all the apparatus, and you've got to indicate to the

Places

The steps in front of Sproul Hall have been named for Mario Savio. The undergraduate library has the popular Free Speech Café.

1964: *Jack Weinberg, Mario Savio, and Suzanne Goldberg, who were among the leaders of the Free Speech Movement. Courtesy of the Bancroft Library of the University of California, Berkeley.*

people who run it, to the people who own it, that unless you're free, the machine will be prevented from working at all."[5]

The university, Weinberg said, had become a dehumanizing machine. Students understood; they wanted a more personalized education and fewer cattle car lectures. Soon they created the Experimental College to educate themselves.

In April 1965, dozens of students were found guilty in a mass trial and fined for trespass and resisting arrest. The prosecutor was Ed Meese, who would later become President Reagan's attorney general. Savio, Weinberg, and many other protesters were jailed.

The movement they had led, however, proved victorious. The campus opened itself to the unfettered political activity that would enliven and bedevil both it and the surrounding town for decades to come.

How Berkeley Rescued the Bay

Kay and Clark Kerr had always dreamed about living in a hillside home with a view of San Francisco Bay. But when they built such a house in 1949 in El Cerrito, Kay didn't like what she saw. "We watched the destruction of the bay from our living room windows," she told an oral historian. "Where there had been a nice wooded cove at Point Isabel, we watched the bulldozers knock off the trees, and level the area, and fill in the little harbor. We watched the garbage fill at Albany."[1]

Like every bayside city, Berkeley had been abusing its bay for years. Raw sewage ran untreated into the bay, creating what folks called "the Big Stench," until the East Bay Municipal Utility District built its first sewage plant in 1951.

The city burned garbage along the shore, briefly hauled it to sea until 1917 when its contract with Signal Steamship Co. "was suddenly terminated by the destruction of the garbage vessel just outside the Golden Gate, with the loss of all hands on board," and then opened a shoreline dump.[2]

Industrialists, meanwhile, had lined the shoreline from the start with soap factories, tanneries, wharves, chemical firms, and even powder works.

Since at least 1922, the year its Chamber of Commerce vowed to work with the city's health department to make Berkeley the healthiest city in the nation, people were complaining that the dump was bad for their health. The city denied it. "The fill is not a rat harbor," Roy W. Pilling, assistant to the city manager, insisted.[3] By 1929, though, the problem was inescapable. Plans to improve Berkeley's long popular bathing beach by building a palatial bath house were scotched when the state's sanitation chief ruled Berkeley's waters "totally unfit for recreational use."[4]

Still, in its 1949 annual report, the city crowed about its landfill: "In the 25 years since the plan was begun, the City's wastes had created acres of useful real estate where only mudflats had existed before."[5]

1949: *Berkeley's waterfront was still open territory in 1949. The lagoon is Aquatic Park. The Berkeley Pier, center, would later be the centerpiece of a large marina. Courtesy of the Berkeley Historical Society, 1.1.1.194 0064.*

By the late 1950s, Berkeley was planning to broaden its industrial base by filling eight hundred acres of the Bay. Similar plans were in the works all around the Bay. Maps showed what the Bay would look like in the future—a river. We would have had a Bay Area without a bay.

By 1961, Kay Kerr had seen her fill, and so had her friends Esther Gulick and Sylvia McLaughlin. Kay's husband was president of the university. Sylvia's was on the Board of Regents. That gave them some sway but not enough. The trio called a meeting of Bay Area conservationists, hoping to hand them the ball. Instead they were told: run with it.

"I didn't have much hope," Harold Gilliam wrote years later. "The odds that such giants," he wrote of the railroad-real estate firms and financial combines that owned much of the bayshore, "with billions of dollars behind them—could be stopped by a handful of starry-eyed bay savers was laughable."[6]

Kerr, McLaughlin, and Gulick began lobbying the Berkeley City Council. And planner Mel Scott produced a report that turned a lot of heads, "The Future of San Francisco Bay."

Berkeley, thanks to a new liberal council majority, was the first city to drop major plans for bayfill. But one victory wasn't enough. "Although we had success in stopping the Berkeley fill," McLaughlin recalled, "it was appalling to find out how many other cities had plans for large bay fills."[7] One project, Westbay, would have flattened San Bruno Mountain to fill most of the South Bay.

Working with veteran San Francisco assemblyman Eugene McAteer, the trio pushed for a strong regulatory body that later became the Bay Conservation and Development Commission. McAteer called on them whenever a show of support was needed. Kerr, Gulick, and McLaughlin would bring busloads of people to Sacramento—and send bags of sand to legislators.

Governor Reagan signed the act into law. "We had persistence," McLaughlin told the interviewer, "and the know-how came by doing."[8]

Saving the bay inspired conservationists worldwide. Locally, it led to successful efforts to preserve open space and creeks. It was, Gilliam wrote, among the first victories anywhere over the "juggernaut of development."[9]

The Save the Bay fight also gave the world a term it will never forget. "The first person I heard use the word 'environment,' in the sense we now know it, was Kerr," Gilliam wrote. He watched her approach the founder of Common Cause after he gave a speech to demand, "Why didn't you talk about the *environment*?" Kerr continued, "He was obviously taken by surprise and could only mumble."[10]

How Berkeley Preserved Its Neighborhoods

Like any city worth living in, Berkeley has always been a city of neighborhoods. And earlier than most cities, Berkeley learned that preserving those neighborhoods takes work from the grassroots up. One of Berkeley's greatest contributions to America is its promotion of neighborhood preservation. The city's efforts to preserve its neighborhoods through rezoning, traffic-calming, and historic preservation have been much emulated elsewhere.

It was in the decades after World War II that American cities were ripped apart by highway building, redevelopment, race riots, the call of newly built suburbs, and white flight. Berkeley after the war was a changed town, with a larger population, grand Victorian homes that had been carved into apartments, streets that had deteriorated, and a shortage of parks. The city, George Petitt wrote, was "tattered and torn."[1]

Traffic increased and parking grew difficult. The Key Route, the East Bay's private commuter rail line, reduced service throughout the 1950s and finally quit in 1958. AC Transit, a public bus agency, took on some of its routes, but trains no longer rolled across the Bay Bridge.

Big plans were in the works for industrial development along the shoreline and for a state highway along Ashby Avenue that would have turned the mainly two-lane residential road into a freeway. The new liberal council of 1961 blocked the shoreline expansion—goaded on by the Save the Bay activists. And residents of working-class and heavily black West Berkeley—allied with people from the affluent Claremont district, which also would have suffered—helped kill the Ashby Freeway.

In 1963, the new council majority provided the neighborhoods with another gift—down-zoning much of flatland Berkeley to ensure that it would remain a city primarily of single-family homes. Eleven years later, voters strengthened this effort by approving a neighborhood preservation ordinance.

Plans by BART, the regional transit agency, to run elevated tracks through the center of town in the early 1960s united both liberals and conservatives. The city council put a bond measure before voters to help pay for burial and set up towers throughout town, showing how tall and ungainly elevated tracks would appear. "Bury the tracks," signs urged. Voters agreed to do so by a remarkable 83 percent majority.

By the start of the 1970s, Berkeley became one of the first cities in America to create a powerful historic preservation

1948: *The last Key Route commuter train ran through downtown Berkeley in November 1948. Photo by Martin J. Cooney for the* Berkeley Daily Gazette. *Courtesy of the Berkeley Historical Society, 573-194-3680.*

organization, with the Berkeley Architectural Heritage Association growing from a group called Urban CARE. A strong landmarks preservation ordinance was passed in 1974.

"The passionate new interest in historical conservation led to a rediscovery of delightful, bizarre or just plain pleasant buildings hitherto taken for granted," architect John Kenyon recalled. "Suddenly the elegant Florentine post office, the Art Deco library and the dignified old frontages

Ozzie Osborne, *proprietor of the soda fountain at the Elmwood Pharmacy, was a much-admired figure whose travails with rent increases convinced city officials to act. Courtesy of the Berkeley Historical Society.*

along Shattuck became precious and reappeared sometimes in oddly sophisticated colors.

"Most encouragingly of all perhaps, old neighborhoods, well protected now from any other rude shock than a major earthquake, have kept improving in charm and quality."[2]

In the 1980s, to preserve such beloved merchants as Ozzie Osborne, who ran a soda fountain in the Elmwood Pharmacy, the council imposed commercial rent control. "A symbol of Berkeley's determination to preserve its quality of life," writer Conte Seely called it.[3]

During the '70s, all eyes were on what *Chronicle* reporter Demian Bulwa would later dub "Berkeley's passionate hate affair with the automobile."[4] Richard Register, an advocate for walkable "eco-cities," turned a dirt-filled car into a mini-farm near his Cedar Street home. By 1975, the city was installing traffic barriers—concrete, wood-planks, or landscape—to keep cars on main thoroughfares.

Berkeley's favorite traffic-calming measure by far, however, was Joseph Charles the Waving Man. A former second baseman with the Lake Charles Yankees and an Oakland longshoreman, Charles donned yellow gloves every day for thirty years and then stood outside his house on busy Grove Street waving at passersby and saying, "Have a good day."

"I enjoyed waving so much I didn't want to quit," Charles told his friend, reporter Martin Snapp.[5] Charles, who died at age ninety-two, a decade after he quit waving, got fan mail from England, Australia, and Germany, was honored by several city "Joseph Charles Days," and deigned to be interviewed by Walter Cronkite.

1970s:

A car became a garden in the late '70s as activists fought to protect neighborhoods from traffic. Courtesy of the Berkeley Historical Society.

c. 1956: *Mayor Laurance Cross, center with pen, helped forge a liberal Democratic alliance between Hills liberals and flatland blacks in the aftermath of Adlai Stevenson's failed presidential campaign. Courtesy of the Berkeley Historical Society, 490-195-2256.*

How Berkeley Became the People's Republic

In 1971, following "the first radical takeover of city government," the new city council refused to pledge allegiance to the flag.[1] The council was soon spending more time on Vietnam and racism in Rhodesia, Republican councilman Thomas McLaren complained, than on city business.

Suddenly, in the national mind, Berkeley emerged not as just another troubled town but as something special—"the People's Republic of Berkeley," a symbol to some of Leftists gone berserk and to others of a town that was courageously facing up to serious societal problems on the local, national, and international levels.

The People's Republic image has, in many minds, never been dispelled, but it hides the fact that Berkeley remains a well-run city.

The radicals were interested in more than symbolism. They passed rent control, declared a moratorium on home demolitions in the flatlands to prevent "ticky-tacky" apartments, and pushed for public ownership of power—an effort that Socialist mayor J. Stitt Wilson pioneered in 1911. They established affirmative action in city hiring and provided low-cost housing, free clinics, and kind treatment for the runaway teens who were flooding Berkeley. They fought for "community control" of police.

How did Berkeley switch from a culturally liberal city with a Republican-dominated government to a city run by liberals and radicals? To outsiders, it seemed to happen overnight, although its roots actually run deep.

After the "radical takeover" of 1971, " the Republicans who had dominated the town since the 1920s seemed to melt away. "Republicans were simply not replaced with Republicans," said David Munstock, a longtime Berkeley progressive.[2]

"We had reached a point in Berkeley history where, in order to be a serious candidate, a politician had to give lip-service to our concerns and to our ideas in the abstract," Loni Hancock wrote about Berkeley's "progressives," formerly known as the "radicals." "The only community debate concerned who could really get it done faster and more responsibly. We were no longer radical in Berkeley. We had become the liberal Democrats."[3]

The progressives' arch-enemy, John DeBonis, an accountant who had served on the council from 1955 to 1971, stewed. "In two years," he predicted in 1973, "the political body unique in the nation, the Berkeley City Council, will have choked its producing citizens to death, just as Vesuvius spewed ash and dust upon the people of Pompeii."[4]

DeBonis can seem a comical figure, as he did to the publishers of "Quotations from Chairman John K. DeBonis," which resembled a famous text by Mao. Here's one quotation: "Everyone knows that the only reason poor women have so many children is because they spend all their time in the bedroom! Bedroom! BEDROOM!"[5]

But DeBonis, who rode with the cops to riots and was a presence on Telegraph Avenue, came across as sympathetic even to many hippies, who called him Johnnie.[6]

How did it come to pass that DeBonis, once a hail and hearty Berkeley city councilman, should become a political outcast? To find out, we need to step back to the end of World War II.

Race had a lot to do with it. Berkeley's black population zoomed from 3,395 at the start of World War II to 21,850 by 1960 . . . 20 percent of the population. And many of the city's

1960s:

Sproul Plaza throughout the '60s saw demonstrations against the war, and over People's Park and ethnic studies. Courtesy of the Berkeley Historical Society, 5-4-4-96-01346.

1980s: *Mayor Gus Newport continued Berkeley's radical tradition in the early 1980s by fighting United States involvement in Central American wars. Photographer Mike Musielski. Courtesy of the Berkeley Historical Society, 4-3-3 1986431.*

preservation, and the need for parks.

In 1947, liberals made an early inroad with the election of Reverend Laurance Cross as mayor. And in 1952, liberals formed the Berkeley Grassrooters after Stevenson's defeat. Berkeley Hills Democrats allied with the black political organization founded by D. G. Gibson and William Byron Rumford, and with blacks who were working for integration of schools and jobs.

In 1958, the liberals elected Jeffery Cohelan to Congress. The liberals' big year came in 1961, when they seized control of the council with five out of the nine members.

The year 1961 also saw the election of Berkeley's first black councilman, Wilmont Sweeney. That election also saw a black man win a seat on the school board for the first time—Reverend Roy Nichols, a leader in the fight for desegregation.

"For the first time in Berkeley's eighty-three-year-old history," the *Gazette* noted, "a Negro will sit on each of the city's two highest ruling bodies."[7] The new council banned housing discrimination for both sales and rentals, integrated the city's workforce, created a welfare commission, built swimming pools, and agreed to save the bay.

The liberal coalition in various forms dominated the council for the rest of the '60s. But it didn't prove an easy ride. Their

conservatives left following the fights over fair housing and school integration in the mid-1960s, convinced that Berkeley was changing in a way they didn't like.

Lowering the voting age to 18, thanks to the 26th Amendment in 1971, also helped push Berkeley to the left. Cal students, who were 4 percent of the population in 1940, were almost 20 percent by the start of the '60s.

Berkeley always had free thinkers. But many of Berkeley's liberals shied away from local politics until stirred up in the late 1940s and early 1950s by anti-Communist hysteria and spurred on by Adlai Stevenson's presidential campaign of 1952.

Many liberals also got involved because of their concern for better urban planning, low-cost housing, neighborhood problems came, however, not from the Right but from the Left. The culprit? A little war in Southeast Asia. "In Berkeley," Joseph Lyford wrote, "Vietnam was a firebomb in a dry forest."[8] Berkeley's liberals, like liberals everywhere, either supported the war or refused to focus on it. But the war came to the council.

Radicals like Bob Scheer, who unsuccessfully challenged Cohelan for Congress in 1966, made the war a make-or-break issue. The shift from liberal pro-war Democrats to antiwar radicals proved as profound as the early shift from Republicans to liberal Democrats.

In 1970, the radical, antiwar city councilman Ron Dellums succeeded in taking out Cohelan in his race for Congress. The war was a big issue. "The first major victory for the radicals," McLaren tut-tutted.[9]

The second major victory came quickly. In 1971, the radicals won four seats on the council—or so it seemed at first—with the election of Loni Hancock, D'Armey Bailey, and Ira Simmons (Bailey's yes-man) to the council, and Warren Widener as mayor.

Bailey, "29, handsome and black," and with a law degree from Yale, pushed for affirmative action programs and for childcare in black neighborhoods.[10] But he took to shuffling like Uncle Tom whenever his path crossed that of his fellow black councilman, Wilmont Sweeney, who wasn't "progressive" enough for him. He called Mayor Widener "the chief pig."[11]

Bailey alienated his white radical supporters and was accused of filibustering "in a manner worthy of a Southern senator."[12] But Bailey was always clear about his goal—"to bring city government to a grinding halt."[13]

Bailey was recalled in 1973 by almost a two-to-one margin—despite Jesse Jackson and the Edwin Hawkins Singers, who rallied to his cause.

By McLaren's count, eighty-nine officers quit the police force in disgust in 1971 and 1972, as radicals demanded "community control" of the police. McLaren called it chaos.[14] Hancock almost agreed. "The years between 1971 and 1973 were my most difficult years on the city council," she wrote, "maybe the the the most difficult years of my life."[15]

The Black Panthers, meanwhile, were running the Bobby Seale People's Free Clinic in South Berkeley and distributing free food. And, two months after murdering Oakland's superintendent of schools, the Symbionese Liberation Army kidnapped Patty Hearst from her Berkeley apartment and brainwashed her into helping them rob sporting goods stores and banks. Most of the SLA would soon be killed in a shootout or arrested—some after detonating various bombs. Hearst was sentenced to federal prison.

But the progressives became the establishment. Since the '70s, they have either dominated the council or traded off with slates of moderate Democrats, which in the early days allied with Republicans. Soon, however, there were few Republicans to ally with.

Anyone watching Berkeley, from within or without, understood that it had become Berkeley. The people it attracted, the people it retained, decided in advance that they were Berkeley people. They were a self-selected bunch. Victims of fate.

The numbers tell the story: in 1962, Berkeley had 31,560 Democrats and 25,068 Republicans. In November 1968, when Nixon beat Humphrey for president, Berkeley had 42,470 Democrats and 17,553 Republicans. In 1972, when Nixon trounced McGovern, Berkeley had 67,151 Democrats and 15,550 Republicans. In 1984, Berkeley had 59,353 Democrats and 10,911 Republicans. By 2005, the rout seemed complete: 43,766 Democrats, 3,747 Republicans.

Yet Berkeley seemed strangely sedate. Loni Hancock, once radical, was a state assembly moderate. Her husband, Mayor Tom Bates, was berated from the left as pro-development and for harassing street people.

How Berkeley Erupted

The protests, sit-ins, teach-ins, moratoriums, and riots that followed America's escalation of the war and the bombing of Cambodia drove even more longtime residents from town.

The late 1960s saw riots and police actions—even occupations by federal troops and tear-gassing by helicopters—over the issue of Vietnam, the Third World Liberation Front's efforts to create a "Third World College," and the university's occupation of People's Park, not to mention the encampments of hippies that occupied much of Telegraph Avenue and assorted open spaces.

"Have you looked at the park on Hearst and Grant lately?" Republican councilman John DeBonis asked. "Do you call *that* beautiful? It's a gypsy land, it's a hobo jungle. Eating their Mulligan stew tonight out of a big ash can. Do you want that in your neighborhood? I'm talking about the hippie Disneyland up there."[1]

By the mid-'60s, action on the street was far outpacing action on the council. Robert Scheer, Jerry Rubin, and, starting in 1965, math professor Stephen Smale led antiwar protests with the Vietnam Day Committee. Berkeley was one of the first cities in America to erupt over the war.

Protesters blocked and boarded trains carrying troops to their debarkation point in Oakland. "It was a wildly confused scene—stretching nearly two miles along the Santa Fe railroad tracks from Berkeley into Albany—at times resembling a guerrilla ambush more than an organized protest," the *Examiner* reported. A street gang from Albany spit on the protesters. "For the most part, the soldiers only smiled at the wild scene—several gave 'V' signs with their fingers."[2]

Opponents of the war sometimes took it out on servicemen, but that wasn't always so in Berkeley. Eric Anthony, a lance corporal who was recovering from his wounds at the base on Treasure Island, had no problem record-shopping on Telegraph Avenue in his dress greens. "People addressed me as 'Sir' in the most respectful tones," he told the *Chronicle* many years later. "It was the only time I walked down Telegraph Avenue without being panhandled every six yards or so."[3]

By the end of the year, Berkeley Women for Peace deluged Lyndon B. Johnson's White House with one hundred thousand Christmas cards demanding peace. The Berkeley Medical Aid Committee sent supplies to the Vietcong.

By 1969, though the university refused to shut for Moratorium Day, more than three thousand turned out for the protest—in the rain. Over the next two years, protests against Vietnam, ROTC, the university's complicity in the war machine, and more convulsed the town, with almost daily protests, walk-outs from school, and mass teach-ins, with Dan Siegel intoning, "the university is just as much the enemy as the Pentagon."[4]

Fires were set at the campus's Life Sciences Building and windows smashed at chancellor Roger Heyn's house. Professors complained of "marauding bands of rock throwers, vandals and arsonists."[5] And there was lots of tear gas. "Five hour 'gas war'

1965: *Protesters tried to block troop trains heading for the Oakland Army Base in August 1965. Courtesy of the Oakland Museum of California/Tribune. Photo by Leo Cohen.*

on and near the UC campus fogged out the sun at times," the *Gazette* reported after one incident.[6]

It was the Third World Liberation Strike of 1969, however, that really drew out the big guns. Black, Hispanic, and Asian student groups demanded ethnic studies. "As sure as hell is hot," Afro-American Student Union leader Jim Nabors said, "there will be a Third World College at the University of California."[7]

Some supporters, many of whom were white, took to racing through the student union, overturning tables and throwing dishes. A bomb was found in Dwinelle Hall. Protesters blocked intersections and got into fistfights with frustrated drivers.

By mid-February, Governor Ronald Reagan had declared a "state of extreme emergency," National Guard helicopters were buzzing above a "war-like campus scene," and three thousand marchers stared at "the largest display of organized law enforcement in Berkeley's history."[8]

"I want to make it clear," Chancellor Heyns insisted, "that the state of emergency, required for technical reasons, does not imply any change in our normal campus life."[9]

In March, Heyns created the Department of Ethnic Studies, one of the first in the nation.

1960s: *National Guardsmen and Highway Patrolmen face down demonstrators at University and Oxford, near the campus. Courtesy of the Oakland Museum of California.*

How Berkeley Went "Berserkeley"

It's easy enough to laugh about Berserkeley. There was Wavy Gravy, dressed like a clown, founder of the Hog Farm. There was Augustus Owsley Stanley, also known as "Bear," who didn't invent LSD but did more than anyone else to commercialize it from his lab in Berkeley in the mid-1960s, "essentially seeding the modern psychedelic movement," according to *Chronicle* writer Joel Selvin.[1]

Berkeley was home to the Fellowship of the Clear Light, a religion with LSD as its sacrament. Berkeley had Hare Krishnas galore and Om the guru, a "bearded black man of perhaps thirty," attended by "a bevy of ardent young followers." He could make traffic lights turn green through willpower, according to Thomas Farber, a denizen of the avenue, who never actually observed this.[2]

The One World Family Commune, which pioneered the soybean "macroburger," ran a cooperative food store, café, dance hall, and the Far Outfits handmade clothing shop on Telegraph in the late sixties and early seventies. Allen Michael, the group's "enlightened being and galactic channel," preached weekly. "The concept of flying saucers, UFOs and extraterrestrials was all new," follower Del Rainer wrote of her introduction to the group. Besides using "an abundance of psychedelics," One Worlders engaged in group tantric sex and put on concerts featuring their house band, Quazar.[3]

And what university town wouldn't have a branch of the Sexual Freedom League? Berkeley's was run by its "maidenhead," Colette, who joined in 1966 because, of all the places she'd ever lived, she said, Berkeley was the hardest to meet men. The *Barb* reported on the League's first nude party. "Though clearly stated as a nude party, the problem that first appeared was how to get people out of their clothes."[4] The answer: play Watusi records!

Seriously though, Wavy Gravy went on to form the Berkeley-based Seva Foundation, which provides medical care in Tibet, Tanzania, and other troubled lands. And Owlsey pioneered modern sound systems for such rock bands as the Grateful Dead, helping destroy as many ears as he had minds.

Stewart Albert didn't see anything funny about "our beloved Free University of Berkeley," which provided "some serious reading and a lot of serious thinking."[5] Courses taught community activism and delved into the Farmer Labor Movement, Latin American development, astrology, and

1970s: *"Hate," as he called himself, danced with the crowd at Provo Park. Courtesy of photographer Kim Cranney.*

1970s: *Conga drummers have been on Lower Sproul Plaza since the sixties. Courtesy of photographer Kim Cranney.*

experimental film. Richard Alpert, also known as Baba Ram Dass, ran a seminar on psychedelics.

Churches, communes, and other groups also took seriously the need to care for the horde of hippies flocking to town, creating the Berkeley Free Clinic and providing free housing. The *Barb* announced in 1966 that free food would be provided every day at Provo Park. "Bring bowl and spoon."[6]

Berkeley remained a city of contrasts. On one night in 1968, seekers of enlightenment could catch LSD guru Timothy Leary, who lived in the Berkeley Hills, at the Berkeley Community Theater, or evangelist Billy Graham at the Greek Theatre. How to choose?[7]

How Berkeley's Telegraph Avenue Suffered

The protests were not all about Vietnam. The war was just a symptom of a rotten society that had to go—in its entirety. In parts of Berkeley, it went. Consider the Telegraph troubles, which lasted from 1968 through 1969 and helped put Berkeley on the national map as a city where anything goes.

Thanks to its reputation developed in the sixties, Telegraph remains a nationwide symbol of live-and-let-live, despite city crackdowns against homeless people sprawled on the sidewalk. It's attracted several generations of proto-punks, post-punks, neo-hippies, hip-hoppers, and occasional Goths, and they keep coming, as do artisans, street musicians, and preachers.

Every hippie in the Bay Area attended the Fourth of July celebration in 1968. Despite pleas from businesses, churches, and the hippies themselves, the city wouldn't close the street for a party. Still, fifteen thousand people crowded in, hanging from rooftops, legs dangling from ledges. They listened to rock bands and watched street theater and fireworks. Temperatures climbed to 90 degrees, but the evening passed peacefully.

But on August 30, also a hot night, kids roamed town after an antiwar rally. Then "a man said by spectators to be in a state

1970s: *A Hare Krishna devotee made his way along Telegraph Avenue in the '70s. Photographer Kim Cranney.*

172

of hysteria" broke a window at the Bank of America on Telegraph Avenue—and the police poured in. Riots followed the next night, a state of emergency declared, and a curfew imposed.[1]

Pat and Fred Cody, whose Cody's Books was a focal point of Telegraph Avenue for decades, described the almost daily "games" between hippies and cops with their tear gas canisters.

"First the gathering of a group, then their darting forward closer to the police, then the rush toward the crowd by the police and the rain of canisters. As these landed and a staccato 'pop,' 'pop,' 'pop' punctuated their arched descent, some were hurled back along with rocks and missiles at charging police. Then, as the police charged, the street was filled with a yelling mass of

A BUSINESS SECTION OF TELEGRAPH AVENUE, BERKELEY, CALIFORNIA   K-197

c. 1940s: *Telegraph Avenue seemed like any commercial street anywhere in the days before World War II. Postcard courtesy of Sarah Wikander.*

hurtling bodies. The police then resumed a stationary position and the pause before the next round began."[2]

The Codys, whose political sympathies were to the left (Pat had helped found Women for Peace in 1961), bristled in 1967 when hippies who set up permanent encampments in front of their door accused Fred of being "a prime example of capitalist rapacity."[3]

Places

The Caffe Med, 2475 Telegraph, remains as welcoming to all comers as it was back in the sixties.

The accuser, a young man named Hajji, served tea and cakes from a samovar gaily arrayed on a Persian rug on the sidewalk. Hajji would often climb a tree, the better to speechify. Once he performed a wedding in front of the bookstore.

Shortly before he was deported, Hajji made his good-byes. "Well, capitalist Cody," he said to Fred, hugging him, "this is a summer you will not forget, eh?"[4]

1983: *A bamboo-flute maker tries out his wares from his spot in front of Cody's Books in 1983. Street merchants have made Telegraph Avenue a tourist spot for decades. Courtesy of the Berkeley Historical Society, 414-198-3506.*

How Berkeley
Battled for a Park

Perhaps nothing better symbolizes Berkeley's pioneering role in shifting power from grand institutions to the community than People's Park. The power was the university, and the community was made up largely of hippies, students, and street people, which only makes the example stronger.

Architect John Kenyon had watched sadly in the mid-1950s as university expansion gobbled up the Southside neighborhood where he lived.

"All around us between 1956 and 1960, great numbers of splendid Shingle Style villas were torn down and replaced by bland shoebox apartment buildings . . . whole frontages of delightful 'obsolescent' houses along Bowditch and Dwight Way, considered a hippie nuisance by the university, were bulldozed down to create a problematic building site that later became the pathetic and ultimately futile People's Park."[1]

Thanks in part to the GI Bill, Cal's enrollment more than doubled between 1945 and 1948 to more than twenty-five thousand. So the university slated the 2.8-acre lot for student housing and then for recreation. But, in fact, the lot sat idle until early 1969, when the community moved in, planted trees and flowers, and built swings and benches. Many slept there.

"The park was our continuous, glorious toy," wrote Stew Albert. "We played all week and like Silly Putty the park changed with our imagination. It was the greatest joy most of us ever gave our labor to—unqualified goodness."[2]

What ensued, however, proved the saddest tale from Telegraph's Troubles—and one of the most historically important. Today, most social theorists would agree with a man named Hate, a resident of the park who spoke to the *Chronicle* nearly forty years after the events in question. "The park is a symbol around the world of people standing up to government," he said.[3]

But that's not how it seemed at the time to Mayor Wallace Johnson, who despaired when he read such missives from People's Park supporters as: "Fight for a revolutionary Berkeley with your friends, your dope, your guns," or "We will make Telegraph Avenue and the South Campus a strategic free territory for revolution."[4]

The university told park supporters to clear out—but also promised not to shut the park without notice. But that's exactly what they did at 3 a.m. on May 15, 1969, "Bloody Thursday," when three hundred cops arrived. With them was Mayor Johnson. "There were no occupants that morning except two or three small males, stoned, sitting in the yoga lotus position," he said.[5] They were lifted by their elbows and removed. By late morning, fifty supporters gathered in the park. Most left when asked; a few were arrested.

Reporter Joe Pichirallo of the *Daily Cal* watched cops loll on the grass and sit on the swings. Crews began fencing off the park at 6 a.m.

At noon, a rally at Sproul Plaza ended when incoming student government president Dan Siegel offered up a few alternatives to a crowd of three thousand. When he came to the alternative "go to the park now," Pichirallo reported, that's all folks needed to hear. Off they went, to be met by police from many jurisdictions.

Someone opened a fire hydrant. A cop trying to close it was stoned from a nearby rooftop. A county sheriff's deputy "immediately whirled around and without warning fired a round of birdshot," Pichirallo reported.[6] Among the hundreds of young people on the roofs were a contingent from

Throughout the afternoon, crowds of people were driven back by police; perhaps three dozen people were hit by shot. "The blood streaming down the faces of participants and observers was not the result of clubbing," Pichirallo wrote, "but was caused by shot from police guns."

Over the next two days, Berkeley was an occupied town. Mayor Johnson went to the hospital to visit Rector, who had lost his spleen, portions of his pancreas and bowels, and left kidney. His heart stopped the next day.

The day after that, three thousand people, who gathered for what was billed as a peaceful day of mourning for Rector, were pepper-gassed by copters. "Up on the Plaza," Stew Albert wrote, "the helicopter was spraying solid white fire into the lungs of sorority girls who never marched in anything but loyalty parades." Weeks of street battles followed.

The city council, liberal though it was, "didn't even have the temerity to tell outside police to stop shooting their citizens," the *Barb* wrote.[8] Councilman Ron Dellums's proposal to send the National Guard home failed for lack of a second. "Even John

the Telegraph Rep cinema, including owner George Pauley and manager Allen Blanchard. Just before the gunshot, the *Berkeley Barb* reported, Blanchard had been "trying to persuade a more violent brother to lay down the brick he was going to throw at the pigs in the street."

Pauley and Blanchard were hit by the deputy's buckshot. Pauley's injuries were relatively minor. Blanchard was hit in both eyes, losing one immediately and losing most of the sight in the other. Others were hit in the torso, chest, and limbs, including James Rector, who was visiting from San Jose. "I guess he didn't duck fast enough," a friend said.[7]

Swingle's innocuous suggestion to have the Guards put the sheaths back on their bayonets failed," the *Barb* said.

But spirits remained high, Albert reported. "You can walk down the Berkeley streets and almost everybody smiles and nods—people will share cigarettes, candy, grass and speculation. We have learned to live existentially—at any moment a lurching pig car pulls up and we

Places

Down from the People's Park, at Telegraph and Haste, is the People's Park mural by Osha Neumann.

are clubbed and arrested—yet we learn to love each other as we stand on our bloody sidewalks and plan revenge."

Almost forty years later, People's Park was still a people's park, complete with a stage, a free-box, pickup basketball games, groves of evergreens, picnickers, avid supporters, and encampments of hippies and homeless.

1960s: *A National Guard copter buzzes above a People's Park protest march. Courtesy of the Oakland Museum of California.*

1970:

The University Art Museum, designed by Mario Ciampi and opened in 1970, was built around a collection of Hans Hofmann paintings donated by the artist. Under director Peter Selz, it became a leading regional museum and home to the Pacific Film Archive. Courtesy of photographer Kim Cranney.

How Berkeley Got Good Taste

The Ohlone Indians who inhabited Berkeley's plains and hills enjoyed oysters, mussels, fish, birds, acorn meal, and deer. The first meal consumed by Europeans in town was recorded by Juan Crespi, who passed through in March 1772. "As soon as we stopped, the soldiers succeeded in killing a bear, so that they had fresh meat to go on with."[1]

Something like a gourmet ghetto emerged in the early 1900s around Dwight Station, where the Southern Pacific trains dropped commuters on Shattuck near Dwight. Husbands hurrying home to wives could pick up "pickles, cooked meats, salads, fruit, etc." from the Original Delicacy Store or choose "something hot for cold weather, hot coffee, hot chocolate, hot bouillon, hot tamales" from the Dwight Way Kandy Kitchen. The Premium Market, a few doors down, offered beef, veal, mutton, and fish.

Folks could grab a bite at the Owl Sandwich and Oyster Grotto, around the corner on Grove Street. And in the morning, the Variety Coffee Company offered a perk-me-up. "Our own roast," the ad in the *Courier* bragged. "Call and see it work. The Best and Freshest Costs No More." Still, not everyone was satisfied.[2]

"Oh for a café," the *Courier* moaned in 1906. "Cheap places there are in plenty, but of the high-class variety there is none."[3]

It would take sixty-five years, some would say, before that began to change—so strong has the myth about Chez Panisse grown. Yes, Chez Panisse, which started in 1971, helped create "California Cuisine." But Berkeley had fine restaurants before Chez Panisse, including Potluck, which began serving informal European dishes on University Avenue in the mid-1950s.

Nor was Chez Panisse the first tenant in the soon-to-be famous Gourmet Ghetto. The real pioneer was Alfred Peet, a Dutch emigrant who'd been in the coffee and tea trade in Holland and Indonesia, and then worked in San Francisco for major importers. He found their wares less than the best. In 1966, a friend from a folk dance class told him about an empty paint store at Vine and Oxford, and Mr. Peet—no one ever called him Alfred—was in business.

"It was a very dull neighborhood then," he told David Darlington two decades later. "There was nothing—a Chinese laundry and an old lady who sold second-hand shopping bags." The Berkeley Co-op and a Safeway store were around the block. Peet neglected to hang a sign. "I put in a little roasting machine. I figured if I roasted it, people could smell it."[4]

Selling by the cup started as a sideline, to convince people that his dark roast was better than the weaker competition. "You call that coffee? Tastes like poison to me," people protested. But Peet's caught on. Early customers tended to be Europeans who understood full-flavored coffee.[5]

Soon the corner of Oxford and Vine was coffee central, where decades of philosophical arguments would be hashed out by overcaffeinated intellectuals while leaning against newspaper racks. Mr. Peet was never among them.

"I've never been a heavy coffee drinker," he told Darlington. "I like to have a little bit of *high quality* coffee that's very strong—that's satisfying—rather than a watered-down version in quantity." In fact, Peet preferred tea. And, although he helped give the folks who created Starbucks their start, he was never fond of the coffee drinks they invented. "You don't make mulled wine with a Chateau La Tour," he groused.

A year after opening, Peet was approached by a couple who thought about starting a cheese shop. "I said, 'Sure, if people

have good taste for coffee it'll be good for cheese, good for wine.' " The Gourmet Ghetto was underway.[6]

Elizabeth and Sahag Avedisian didn't know much about cheese—but neither did anyone else. Customers were enthusiastic, studied up, and were hired. "After about six months of talking and eating, and hanging out with Sahag and Elizabeth, I started working there," said L. John Harris, a pioneering Cheese Boarder who later became a food writer and filmmaker.[7]

In 1971, just as Chez Panisse was opening, Cheese Board was sold to its employees and turned into a cooperative. By that time, it had one of the best selections in the country. The Cheese Board was soon baking its own bread and mak-

1975:
Alice Waters turned her attention to tarts, c. 1975. Courtesy of Chez Panisse.

Places
The Gourmet Ghetto is centered on Shattuck and Vine.

ing its own pizzas. The grassy Shattuck Avenue median out front became one of Berkeley's top picnic spots.

Just as Peets welcomed the Cheese Board, the Cheese Board welcomed Chez Panisse—in its own way. "I know I will never forget the astonishing night in the seventies," Chez Panisse founder Alice Waters recalled, "when the merry collectivists, having stripped themselves naked, burst through our front door in the midst of dinner service and streaked through the restaurant, the very embodiment of ecstatic, anarchic nature, if not anarcho-syndicalism."[8]

Begun as something informal but very French—Waters and partners hired waiters who really were French—Chez Panisse gradually became Californian by focusing on locally grown ingredients simply but carefully prepared. It was an innovation that chef Jeremiah Tower, first a follower and later a rival, claimed as his own.[9]

Waters, her boyfriend David Lance Goines, a poster artist who had been involved with the Free Speech Movement, and Tom Luddy, head of the Pacific Film Archive, were part of what the *Chronicle* called a "loosely knit, left of center, artistic-culinary salon."[10]

From the start, Chez Panisse was as much crusade as restaurant, trying to convince people that this was the best way to eat. Like Frances Moore Lappé, author of *Diet for a Small Planet*, another Berkeleyan who cared deeply about food and society, Waters approached dining from a socially conscious angle.

The emphasis on education—teaching people to appreciate the finer things in life, to enjoy the good life—was common to many of the denizens of the Gourmet Ghetto, including Peet and the owners of the Cheese Board.

Commentators noted how many folks at Chez Panisse and its rapidly expanding brood of offspring were former academics—in linguistics, architecture, French, education. "A growing number of restaurants," Ruth Stein wrote in 1975, ". . . are being run by former grad students and professionals who have discovered they would rather slave long hours over a hot stove than push papers around or endure the rigors of academia."[11]

It took years for Chez Panisse to become a borrow-money-from-your-parents sort of place, a place that President Bill Clinton would visit along with twenty Secret Service agents. Fellow diners gave him a standing ovation.

In the early days, *Examiner* food critic Stan Sesser recalled, "You could call Alice Waters at 6 p.m., ask her what was cooking that night, and come over oblivious of what you were wearing. For many years a full course dinner was $6.50."[12]

How Berkeley Invented the Hot Tub

Sitting in a hot tub beneath the stars while sipping chardonnay may be associated in the public mind more with Marin County or Malibu than with Berkeley. Hot tubs seem too sybaritic for Berkeley—not challenging enough. But it was in Berkeley that the modern hot tub—complete with spritz—got its birth. Remember how Berkeley invented the good life?

The Jacuzzi Co., founded in West Berkeley in 1915 by a family of Italian emigrants, produced airplane propellers. The firm had its greatest success with irrigation pumps. But its name never became synonymous with a product until fifteen-month-old Kenneth Jacuzzi, who was born in 1941, came down with rheumatoid arthritis. His father, Candido, took a look at the prescribed hydrotherapy bath and decided, "Why, that's just a pump!"[1] He built a submersible pump to use at home between his son's regular therapy sessions.

By the mid 1950s, they were marketing the Jacuzzi for recreational use, using Jayne Mansfield for their spokeswoman. By 1968, the pumps were incorporated in freestanding units, and the Jacuzzi as we know it was born. By the mid-1970s, the hot tub had become a lifestyle, appearing on live-oak shaded decks everywhere and in health spas—including Berkeley's Holistic Health Center on College Avenue, which, like many of its brethren, branched out into such "healing arts" as herbology and "psychic awareness."

"Interest is tremendous," manager Edward Bauman bragged.[2]

How Berkeley Found Its Sound

Music has always marked Berkeley's changes of life. As far back as 1886, the editors of the student yearbook *Blue and Gold* focused on sound to note the town's evolution into a city. "The howl of the coyote is seldom heard by the belated student; in its place he hears perhaps the Berkeley Choral Society as it rehearses one of its delightful concerts."[1]

Leading composers have made their mark in town. Charles Seeger, who chaired the music department at the university from 1912 to 1918 and fathered Pete, turned his home into a recital hall. Cal played an important role in electronic and experimental music at its Center for New Music and Audio Technologies, which has operated a pleasant concert hall north of campus.

Berkeley has had hundreds of off-campus classical aggregations over the years, from string quartets to the Berkeley Symphony, which won fame for contemporary performances under Kent Nagano, musical director from 1978 to 2008.

Rhythm-and-blues made its mark, thanks to West Berkeley native Johnny Otis, who headed orchestras, recorded rock 'n' roll hits ("Willie and the Hand Jive") and discovered such stars as Etta James. Otis rounded out his career by promoting jazz and R&B as a KPFA disc jockey and through a class at the local city college.

And trumpeter Phil Hardymon created a trend-setting jazz education program at Berkeley High School in the mid-1960s. Later, the independent Jazz School provided education and concerts.

Berkeley had its psychedelic bands, like Country Joe and the Fish, and its punk scene on Gilman Street. During the 1980s, thanks to the folk-dancing hall Ashkenaz, African and World Beat bands did well.

In 1975, Berkeley became a center for multicultural performance when exiles from Chile and their American supporters founded La Peña. The concept was modeled on the *peñas* that were centers for musical life in Chile before the Allende regime was crushed by an American-backed coup.

La Peña has presented orchestras and dance groups from around the world, sponsored a popular annual festival of "New Song," the Encuentro del Canto Popular, and has become a gathering spot for social and political events. Cesar Chavez celebrated his fiftieth birthday at La Peña, and Dolores Huerta, also a farmworkers leader, her seventieth.

Berkeley's favorite music could well be folk—in the term's broadest sense. Starting in 1957, Berkeley became part of the national folk revival, thanks to Barry Olivier's Berkeley Folk Festival, which ran through 1970.

By the mid-1960s, clubs like the Jabberwock, Blind Lemon ("a cheap, happy place"), Steppenwolf, and New Orleans House were presenting folk and rock almost nightly, and Finnish Brotherhood Hall was a venue for dances. Arhoolie Records, founded in the early 1960s by Chris Strachwitz, spurred the folk and blues revival by recording musicians throughout the South.

Berkeley was also home to Malvina Reynolds, "the Muse of Parker Street." A Cal PhD in English from 1939, Reynolds, who

1970s: *Guitarist and stringed-instrument repairman Campbell Coe was a guru in the 1970s for Berkeley's burgeoning folk and country music scene. Courtesy of the Berkeley Historical Society/photo by Sandy Rothman.*

won fame for her song "Little Boxes (Made of Ticky-Tacky)," began writing folk songs in the 1940s as part of union organizing efforts.

And Berkeley developed a remarkable Old Timey, bluegrass, and Cajun scene, many of whose stars were women. Laurie Lewis pioneered a bluegrass scene "where it's no longer an oddity to find a ballsy woman playing or singing lead."[2] Soon Berkeley was awash with bluegrass and Old Timey bands, including Any Old Time String Band, Grant Street String Band, and the Arkansas Sheiks, many fronted by or featuring women players.

1995: *Dr. Loco (Jose B. Cuellar), who usually played with his Rockin' Jalapeño Band, performed in front of La Peña. Courtesy of La Peña.*

When Lewis and Kathy Kallick put together their all-woman band Good Ol' Persons, Kallick said, "We did know going in that people were going to say, 'Whoa! Five girls are going to try to play bluegrass, that's going to be weird.'"[3]

One of their favorite venues was Freight and Salvage, Berkeley's longest-lasting folk club, founded in 1968. The club has featured hoot nights, blues stars, country stars, and even the occasional avant-garde performer. What there wasn't was booze. "They were

1978: *Kent Nagano during his first season as musical director with the Berkeley Symphony, performing at Lawrence Hall of Science. Courtesy of the Berkeley Historical Society.*

into listening," Laurie Lewis said. "It was definitely a coffee and brownies crowd."[4]

How Berkeley Discovered Yuppies

ike mutant rats they multiply," she warned, announcing a peril few had as yet contemplated, "the YUPs, Young Urban Professionals. Can we survive the plague of the baby boom generation?"

It makes sense that Berkeley, which gave the world hot tubs (if not chardonnay), also invented yuppies. That's not entirely certain, however.

Alice Kahn, who sounded the warning in June 1983 in the *East Bay Express*, may not have invented the term—*Chicago Tribune* columnist Bob Greene used it early on, and so did Jerry Rubin. But Kahn "probably deserves the credit (or the blame)," Bruce J. Schulman wrote in his tome, *The Seventies: The Great Shift in American Culture, Society, and Politics.*

Kahn focused her ire on people in their thirties whose consumption of all things expensive and decadent drove up prices for the rest of us and devastated neighborhoods by replacing mom-and-pop hardware and shoe stores with "sweet stations, gelatos, chocolate heavens, French bakeries."[1]

Her moral high tone was extremely Berkeley. And Kahn had the good taste to describe the quasi-fictional yuppie couple featured in her essay as living not in Berkeley but in Piedmont.

Kahn meant to skewer yuppies, not praise them. She cer-

tainly didn't see them as something to emulate. She proposed a "Yuppie Abatement District," after all.

But marketers took yuppies seriously. "Detroit's New Goal—Putting Yuppies in the Drivers Seat," *Business Week* reported the next year, Schulman revealed.

This may be why Kahn—a member of the Berkeley Women's Health Collective who became a writer to educate people about health—quit work as a columnist for the *Chronicle* and returned to nursing.

But satire was something she never regretted. "I felt I couldn't be flamboyant and goofy as a nurse practitioner," she said, "but I sure could be as a writer."[2]

Places

Yuppies can be spotted along Berkeley's chic Fourth Street shopping district.

How Berkeley Invented Disability Rights

erkeley has kinda, sorta invented many things. But among those things that undisputedly were invented in Berkeley, disability rights stands out for its importance. Today it is largely taken for granted that people using wheelchairs or walkers, or those who cannot see or hear, should be able to get inside buildings, use trains and buses, and attend concerts and films.

But that wasn't so back in 1972, when what is probably the world's first curb-cut—"the slab of concrete heard 'round the world"—was installed downtown at the northwest corner of Shattuck and Center Street.[1]

Many of the federal laws that require accessible restaurants, stores, transit, and housing were devised in Berkeley by people associated with the Center for Independent Living and its offshoots. Hale Zukas, CIL's public affairs specialist, fought for and helped write regulations that later became the Americans with Disabilities Act, which took effect in 1992.

In the late seventies, Zukas—a persuasive man, even though his speech could barely be understood because of cerebral palsy—argued as a member of a federal panel on "architectural barriers" that train stations across the country should be remodeled to allow access for wheelchair users. Government officials smiled indulgently. Too costly, they said. Never will happen. But it happened.

More importantly, the concept behind those laws and the changes in public attitude that have followed were developed in Berkeley by a group of strong-willed cripples.

Still, when Ed Roberts, "the Gandhi of the disability rights movement," spoke about his life in a deep way, it wasn't about curb cuts or Section 504 of the Rehab Act.[2] It was about sex. To Roberts, after all, as to many of his followers, the struggle was about enjoying life to its fullest—a very Berkeley kind of attitude.

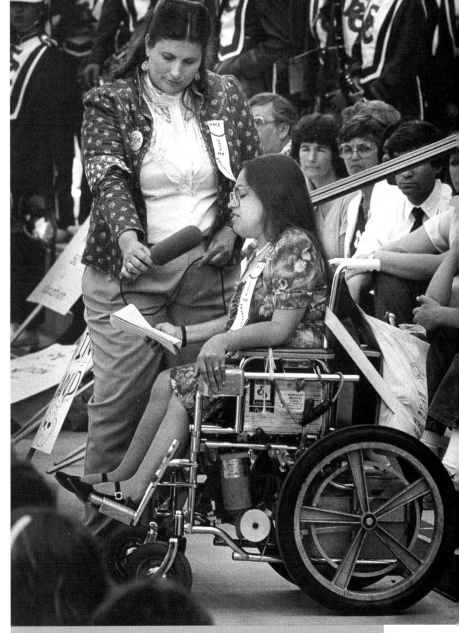

1970s: *Judy Heumann spoke at a rally for special education in the late 1970s. Courtesy of photographer Jon McNally and the Center for Independent Living.*

1970s: *Ed Roberts, CIL's founder, needed extra oxygen often, but he didn't let that stop him from getting things done or enjoying life. Courtesy of the Center for Independent Living.*

"Do you know that some disabled people have never enjoyed a single success in their lives?" Roberts told one reporter. "That there are disabled people put away in institutions right now that have never enjoyed the simple warmth and camaraderie of a family meal around a table?"[3]

Roberts, a junior high school athlete, spent two years in an iron lung after coming down with polio. "Maybe we should hope he dies," a doctor told Ed's mother, "because if he lives he'll be nothing more than a vegetable."[4]

Throughout his life, Roberts spent much of his time in an iron lung, due to a damaged diaphragm—"recharging myself," he said. To accommodate Roberts, the university turned a campus hospital ward into a dorm. Soon other disabled students followed, and Roberts helped create the Physically Disabled Students Program.

At Cal in the late '60s—the years of protest—he studied political science, having already mastered many of its moves. "Everywhere along the way," he told the *Gazette*, "I had to battle. As I won each of those battles I gained confidence in my ability to take on people or systems, and that was pretty important."[5]

But it wasn't till years later, he told the *Examiner*'s Burr Snider, when Roberts saw that women could be interested in him as a man, that "I began to really care about myself and feel value about myself." His occupational therapist, attracted, she said, by "his tremendous ability to reach out with his voice," was soon showing up for therapy in low-cut blouses and miniskirts. Roberts, whose control over his limbs was slight, flirted by winking.

"So much sex is in your head," Roberts told a reporter. "I can feel all over . . . so I can have all the normal reactions and get turned on like any man."[6]

When Roberts wasn't winking, he put together the first organization in America—probably the world—that was run by and for disabled people with the goal of independent living. "Disabled people should run and control any organization created to serve their needs," the organization announced.

Starting in 1972 in a two-bedroom apartment, the Center for Independent Living (CIL) helped disabled people find places to live, on their own or with attendant care, locate jobs, and obtain job training.

Public bus and train operators whose vehicles couldn't handle disabled people soon heard about it. "Boy, do we work on transportation," Zukas told a reporter with his devilish grin. "We're suing everybody in the world."[7]

CIL founded a shop to repair and redesign wheelchairs and other tools for independent living, including equipment that let people without limbs drive cars.

Vance Grippi, who decried the old "Here's a wheelchair; take it or leave it" attitude, made it his life's work to design the perfect wheelchair. "Wheelchairs, understand, are their legs," he explained.[8]

Over the years CIL received federal funding as a "demonstration program," and CIL's programs and philosophy have been copied worldwide. For years, thanks to CIL, curb cuts, relatively accessible transit, and other programs pushed by the center, Berkeley, and environs attracted many disabled people.

"People are literally flocking here from all over the country," CIL's housing director Jerry Woolf, said in the late '70s. "They are landing at the airport and calling us up. About once a month, someone pulls up outside in a taxi and says, 'Here I am!'"[9]

Places

A sidewalk plaque marks the spot of the world's first curb cut on the northwest corner of Center and Shattuck.

How Berkeley
Women Grew Uppity

I f you were a Berkeley female in the sixties, it was easy to scoff at all the jabber about liberation.

"These radical men," Lisa Gerrard wrote, "so self-righteous about the moral superiority of their politics, their opposition to an undeclared war in Southeast Asia, to the oppression of people of color at home and abroad, so quick to label a conservative professor or senator a fascist, thought nothing of forcing their will, not to mention their muscle, on the women they wanted to bed. The pressure ranged from hectoring to downright rape."[1]

Berkeley may not have pioneered women's liberation, but the early 1970s saw the rise of a lively women's community and some trendsetting work in academe.

The Civil Rights Act of 1964 had banned job discrimination on the basis of sex, and the National Organization of Women had been founded two years later. And everybody had read Betty Friedan's *The Feminine Mystique*—except men. As a graduate student in English, Gerrard heard professors joking—it was joking, wasn't it?—about having cute grad students sit in their laps.

Bridget Connelly remembered crying back in 1966 and almost dropping out of grad school when a professor dismissed her as "too ambitious" for taking her studies seriously. "Getting angry hadn't occurred to me," she wrote. "Neither had a feminist perspective."[2]

The comparative literature department, student Deborah Ellis decided, vented its hostility toward women by punishing those bold enough to become mothers. She recalled one

graduate student: "The day after she gave birth she was back at work, leaning against the walls of the corridor as she staggered to her classroom. This was the heroic model offered to those of us looking down at a ten-year doctoral program."[3]

And Cal had few women professors—a total of fifteen in 1970, according to an Academic Senate report. When Doris Earnshaw, who later wrote *The Female Voice in Medieval Romance Lyric*, protested that Cal taught almost no women poets, she was told, "Women don't write poetry. Women make babies."[4]

No wonder women in English and comparative literature, adorned with "Uppity Woman" buttons, were soon reclining on cushions in the apartment of Marsha Hudson, who put herself through school dancing topless while dreaming about a women's studies department.

Literature students weren't the only women getting uppity. At Boalt Hall in 1970, law and sociology students held a Women Breaking the Shackles conference. The Women's Liberation Newsletter argued for legalized abortion that year, and in Albany, the Women's Liberation Basement Press published the article "Sisters in Oppression: a Perspective and a Study."

A women's center for abused women opened that year, and the Flashy Film Co. held weekly screenings. The Rape Project collected women's stories of rape and, "if they haven't repressed it—their experiences of molestation as a child." KPFA inaugurated its women's program in 1971. There was soon a women's coffeehouse across from campus and a free women's university with classes on natural food, mechanics, handicrafts—and a women's action group.

Women took to the street to demand funding for welfare and women's services. "A pinch-in was also planned for last Saturday on Telegraph Avenue," the *East Bay Feminist Newsletter* reported. "Just letting the guys know how it feels." The paper added: "Keep alert for news of a 'pee-in' planned for coming weeks to protest pay toilets for women."[5]

In 1971, Berkeley women "turned the tables on the catcalling men outside the Forum Café on Telegraph Avenue," wrote Deirdre Lashgari, another member of "Marsha's Salon." "Whenever a lone man walked by, they called out 'Ooo baby, swing those balls!' The men invariably looked around in terror, then broke into a run."[6]

Back at the comp lit department, the women from Marsha's Salon found surprising success—in part, no doubt, because the university was under court order. In 1971, the federal Office of Civil Rights ruled that the university was discriminating against women.

Soon the women in comp lit were allowed to create and teach their own courses—Women and Madness, Third World Women, The Devil's Handmaiden: Demonic Women in Literature, etc. "The selections on the reading list represent violence against oneself, against others, and against society," the course description for Women and Violence read. "The very act of writing can have a violent character."

By 1976, Cal had its own women's studies department— one instance where Berkeley was no pioneer. According to Gloria Bowles, the department's first coordinator, more than seventy universities across the country had beaten Cal to it.

How Berkeley's Gays Held Hands

In 1983, a year after founding the East Bay's first gay political club, Armond Boulay looked on the bright side of things. "It shows that the Oakland and Berkeley area is a very mature and sophisticated area if it took a whole year to get our first hate mail," he said.[1]

The East Bay Lesbian/Gay Democratic Club, which was founded a mere eighteen years after the first such group in San Francisco, had just thrown the first gay pride march in Berkeley, attracting four thousand people, a fine turnout. San Francisco's parade, a week later, attracted two hundred thousand.

Gay life runs deep in Berkeley—though often silent. Robert Duncan, who grew up in Oakland and studied at Cal in the late '30s, wrote an early argument for treating homosexuals as a minority group that deserved civil rights in his essay "The Homosexual in Society." Back in Berkeley after World War II, Duncan became the center of a poetry scene later called the Berkeley Renaissance.

"It was sometimes obscene, sometimes homoerotic," Dinitia Smith wrote in the *New York Times* of the work of Duncan, Jack Spicer, and their friends.[2] They would attend soirees chez Duncan, where the poet, "functioning as shaman of an emerging literature grounded in magic, polytheism, and sexual diversity," would be "borne into the living room on pillows," according to Texas poet Paul Christensen.[3]

Another Cal graduate, Phyllis Lyon, helped found America's pioneering lesbian organization, the Daughters of Bilitis, in 1955. Not surprisingly, most of its activities took place across the bay in San Francisco.

Gay activism heated up at the start of the 1970s with Gay Liberation Front and Gay Student Union dances at Pauley Ballroom. The most important event from this period was the founding in 1973 of the Pacific Center for Human Growth, a community and social services center for gays and, later, bisexual and transgender people, which provided crucial help once AIDS hit.

Berkeley passed a pioneering ordinance banning discrimination against gays in housing or employment. The ordinance came in the wake of Anita Bryant's campaign in Florida to ban gays from teaching. The Brick Hut, a Berkeley café run and frequented largely by lesbians, reacted to Bryant's proposal in its own way—by refusing to pour orange juice, a product Bryant promoted in TV spots.

And Berkeley did beat San Francisco to the punch on one important matter. In December 1984, it became the first city in the United States to pass a domestic partners law, giving city employees in gay partnerships the same benefits as married couples.

Still, Berkeley never attained San Francisco's allure. Student Rembrandt Flores spoke for many when he told the *Daily Cal* in 1995, "If I want to do something gay, I usually go to the city."[4]

Berkeley's failure to attract gays seeking entertainment was also tied to homophobia. Don Pharoah was out enough in 1987 to chair the Gay and Lesbian Democratic Club's political action committee—but not to hold his lover's hand in public. He told the *Oakland Tribune* he was attacked on campus for being gay.[5]

At the start of the 1990s, Cal was teaching lesbian, gay, bisexual, and transgender studies—finally joining Harvard, Yale, Rutgers, Duke, San Francisco State, and others. By 1997, a dorm floor had been reserved for gay students, a first in the Cal system. "It's hard to be the only gay person on your floor," student Randy Althouse told the *Tribune*. "Here, you feel part of a community. It's been a great comfort to me."[6] Still, one night someone stood outside shouting over and over, "Queers!"

The East Bay chapter of Queer Nation, meanwhile, took to riding the rails in the early '90s, squeezing onto crowded BART trains headed for the suburbs and making out. "Don't you feel bad when you make someone squirm?" one rattled commuter asked.[7]

Places

The Pacific Center is at 2712 Telegraph Avenue.

In 1998, the city council stopped providing the Sea Scouts with a free berth at the Berkeley Marina for its training vessel because of the Boy Scouts' policy against gays. The local scout organization was fine with gays—it was the first in the country to defy the Scouts' ban on gay members—but not the national. And that was enough for Berkeley.

From the early 1970s, Berkeley became a welcoming place for lesbians in the know, who flocked to several bars and restaurants mostly south of campus and in North Oakland. The Brick Hut, originally "two booths and five stools at the counter," began as a nine-woman co-op across from the Ashby BART station and was immortalized as the cover shot on an album by singer Mary Watkins.

Known for the community it created as well as for its food—fans happily waited two hours for breakfast—the Brick Hut moved to San Pablo Avenue near Dwight in the 1990s, adding to that neighborhood's reputation as a mini-gay district. Soon, at the suggestion of Brick Hut's owners, a woman's bookstore opened a branch store alongside Good Vibrations, which sold sex toys. Lesbians and gays, some moving from the city, bought up homes near San Pablo Park in what was largely a black neighborhood. Some called it "Girl Town."

When the Brick Hut went bankrupt in 1997, people mourned.

How Berkeley Indians Rallied 'Round Their Sacred Ground

T he Huchiun people and their kin lived for four thousand years along Berkeley's shoreline and creeks, and among its oak groves. But the Europeans who followed did what they could to remove their traces. Wilhemine Bolsted Cianciarulo, who grew up in West Berkeley during the 1880s and '90s, remembers seeing shellmounds just past Second Street, by "a beautiful beach of white sand."

"When the mounds were removed to make way for the present-day factories, many Indian skeletons, stone utensils, and arrowheads were found," she wrote. "The gruesome things were given to our University for study."[1]

About 425 shellmounds—up to nine meters high and 183 meters in diameter—once dotted the Bay Area, many along the shore or alongside creeks or estuaries, Cal archeologist Nels Nelson determined in the early twentieth century. Even then, they were disappearing quickly, thanks to development, despoilment, and mining. In 1909, Nelson observed, "Not a single mound of any size is left in its absolutely pristine condition."[2]

Ads in the Berkeley Gazette offered phosphate-rich material from an "Indian burial mound," "one of the finest of fertilizers."

In the early days, archeologists regretted the loss of important historical sites. Places where Indians lived and worked revealed what little we know about the Bay Area's original ancestors—that, plus some revealing reports left by the Spanish padres and soldiers who had cajoled and often corralled the local tribes into moving to the Missions. Thousands of Mission Indians died of diseases imported by their Spanish overseers.

The mounds revealed what the Indians ate (shellfish, immense sturgeon, harbor seals, birds, elk, and deer), what

Remains of a Native American inhabitant discovered in a shellmound. Courtesy of the Berkeley Historical Society.

tools they used (stone pestles, mortars, drills, axes, hammers, knives, and arrowheads), how they dressed, and how they were buried. The mounds also showed that Indians engaged in trade over hundreds of miles with fellow tribes.

Besides the shellmounds, the Berkeley Hills are dotted with Indian sites—including Indian Rock and Mortar Rock, two parks that contain deeply incised mortars used by Indians for grinding acorns.

The university emerged early on as a leading center for Indian studies. Besides Nelson and his fellow archeologists, anthropologist Alfred Kroeber catalogued the state's Indians in his *Handbook of the Indians of California*, and befriended Ishi, last of the Yahi Indians. Kroeber's wife, Theodora, immortalized Ishi in her popular book *Ishi in Two Worlds*. Berkeley researchers have also helped record, preserve, and teach Californian Indian languages.

But it wasn't until Native Americans got involved with preserving their ancient culture that things heated up. For the Indians, preservation was more than an academic matter; it was about their ancestors and their culture.

Efforts in the late 1990s to build a shopping center in West Berkeley were fought by Native American activists and preservationists from the Berkeley Architectural Heritage Association. In 2000, the city landmarked the site, which was buried beneath a parking lot near Spenger's Restaurant.

Scientists had fueled the preservationists' efforts by focusing on shellmounds not as mere "trash dumps" but as important sites for ceremonies, dances, and political meetings. Some, according to Edward Luby, Clayton Drescher, and Kent Lightfoot (a Cal anthropologist) were "mounded villages" built atop centuries of animal bones, shells—and human remains.

"They deserve our respect and our protection," Lightfoot said

of the shellmounds, "as places where the first people in the Bay Area lived and died."[3] Lightfoot, an anthropologist, served as curator of the university's Phoebe A. Hearst Museum of Anthropology.

Activists also demanded that the university return to their descendants the hundreds of remains that had been excavated earlier in the century from the mounds.

In 2006, when the university decided to build an athletic training center next to Memorial Stadium, some Indian activists and environmentalists fought the project by camping out in a grove of live oaks that stood in the way. "They want to build a gym where my ancestors are buried," said Zachary Running-Wolf, a Native American who had recently run for mayor.[4] University officials argued that there was no convincing evidence of Native American burials at the site.

Efforts to save about forty oaks—one of them hundreds of years old, the rest planted after the stadium was built in

1923—attracted Country Joe McDonald, the California Oak Foundation, councilwoman Betty Olds, and the ninety-one-year-old Sylvia McLaughlin—who had helped save the bay half a century before and soon found herself perched in a tree—along with a gaggle of tree-sitters who turned the grove into a treehouse city.

Oak lovers, who included a girl named Lizard, a guy named Aquaman, and Doctress Neutopia, were soon chanting

2006: *A mural portraying Huchiun Ohlone Indians was created by artist John Wehrle at University Avenue and Fourth Street, across from one of Berkeley's largest shellmounds, whose remains are hidden by the parking lot at Spenger's Restaurant. Courtesy of John Wehrle.*

hui_i_tak

"om" while doing "the spiral dance," staring each other in the eyes all the while. "Before you leave," Aquaman told a reporter, "spend some time with the trees and really get to know them." Even nudes scrambled up. "I never turn down a chance to take off my clothes," said Debbie Moore, a founder of the X-plicit Players.[5]

The university, which vowed to plant three trees for every one it downed, fenced the grove off for Homecoming, when thousands of football fans from Tennessee padded past. Many enjoyed the tree-sitters. Others were aghast. "This wouldn't happen in Tennessee," Marcus Hilliard told a reporter. "No, ma'am."[6]

Places

A mural by John Wehrle shows Berkeley's Huchiun people; it's across from the shellmound buried beneath Spengers' parking lot. Indian and Mortar Rock parks in the Berkeley Hills preserve mortars used to grind acorns. The Phoebe Apperson Hearst Museum of Anthropology on campus has a vast collection of artifacts and human remains excavated in the East Bay.

2006: *Protesters took to the trees to prevent the university from downing a grove of trees said to be a Native American habitation site. Courtesy of photographer Matthew Taylor.*

How Berkeley Turned Green

In 2005, the owners of Power Bar came up with a great way to celebrate Berkeley's commitment to the environment—a 350,000-pound blue quartzite sculpture showing Berkeley-born-and-bred David Brower, a longtime Sierra Club director and Earth First founder.

Mayor Tom Bates liked it but no one else did. "The notion of a white man astride the globe and reaching for the stars," Richard Brenneman wrote, "evoked images of imperialism for many critics."[1]

The statue may have been deep-sixed, but not so the David Brower Center. The center, "a hub for progressive activism," provided offices for environmental groups, an auditorium and conference center, and a restaurant devised with the help of Alice Waters, who served "affordable organic food harvested from local farms."[2]

Berkeley's environmental roots run deep—at least to John Muir, through the involvement of Berkeleyans with the Sierra Club and state and national parks, and through the work of Brower, who pioneered a militant anti-growth stance.

Berkeley pioneered curbside recycling, thanks to the non-profit Ecology Center in 1973, one of the first curbside collections in the country. Businesses that rescued trash from landfills by converting it into collectibles formed a mini-green business district in West Berkeley.

Berkeley was perhaps the first city in the country to ban the use of Styrofoam containers by restaurants or vendors of take-out food. The 1989 ordinance also banned other ozone-depleting compounds.

In the first decade of the 2000s, when global warming emerged as a threat, Berkeley became one of the first cities in the nation to power a building (the Shorebird Nature Center) with a wind turbine. The city soon required residents to build with green materials and to cut back on packaging, and advised them to take the bus. Plans were underway to subsidize residential solar panels.

Achieving the city's goal—reducing greenhouse gases by 80 percent—might prove expensive and even painful, said Cisco DeVries, who helped devise the plans. "But if Berkeley's niche isn't leadership on this issue, then what is it?"[3]

But it was up the hill, at Lawrence Berkeley National Laboratory, that the most ambitious work was taking place. Lab director Steven Chu, a Nobelist in physics, mounted a campaign against impending global catastrophe with the same urgency that motivated Cal scientists sixty years before when they raced to develop the atom bomb.

The campaign against global warming developed along several fronts, including developing biofuels to replace petroleum—without generating additional carbon pollution or decreasing the world's food supply by turning cropland into fuel farms. Another, one close to Chu's heart, focused on solar energy.

Organizationally, too, the effort was varied. Cal reached a deal with the oil giant British Petroleum and the University of

Illinois to create the Energy Biosciences Institute—the largest industry-sponsored university research ever. Another effort, Helios, was a partnership between UC Berkeley and Lawrence Berkeley Lab. There was also a Joint BioEnergy institute that partnered with several universities and private research firms.

The city created training programs to prepare residents for an upsurge in "green" jobs.

"I think there really is a possibility that UC Berkeley and Lawrence Berkeley National Laboratory could be one of the intellectual centers of the world," Chu announced.[4]

There were, of course, naysayers—this being Berkeley, after all. Many faculty and students worried about the ethics of partnering with a giant oil company like BP and about academic freedom. "Where some of the researchers are con-

cerned, and where I'm concerned," said Henry Stern, a law student with the Berkeley Energy Research Collaborative, "is too much of the research will be appropriated before it's public."[5]

"I didn't enroll in BP-UC," one protester's T-shirt proclaimed.[6]

The battle against the BP deal harked back to associate professor of microbiology Ignacio Chapela's fight a few years earlier against the university's partnership with the biotech firm Novartis. Chapela argued that genetically modified corn developed at the university could infect native corn. His research was called into question by, among others, representatives of agribusiness; Chapela had to sue the university to receive tenure, after a battle that stirred passions worldwide.

But Chu, a can-do sort, refused to apologize for his capitalist strategy. "Moving fast is better than maintaining purity," he said. "Monasteries are good places, but they're not good for science."[7]

Berkeley's Scientific Triumphs

In the 1930s, John Lawrence, Ernest's brother, developed nuclear medicine at the university's radiation lab.

In the years after World War II, thanks in part to Lawrence Berkeley Lab and its oversight of Los Alamos and Lawrence Livermore Lab, Cal scientists pioneered research and developments in nuclear physics, biology, nanotechnology, and more. Important advances in superconductors and compact fluorescent lighting were made at the Lab. Berkeley was also part of the consortium that mapped the human genome.

The technique of carbon-dating was developed at Berkeley, as was the chemical laser and an algorithm used to prevent gridlock on the Internet. The mechanisms behind photosynthesis were elucidated here. Berkeley scientists discovered sixteen elements, including, of course, berkelium.

2006:

Physicist Steven Chu, director of the Lawrence Berkeley Laboratory, mounted a crash campaign to stave off environmental degradation. Courtesy of the Lawrence Berkeley National Laboratory.

How Berkeley Worried

By 2007, even the good news had a dark side. "All those organic bean sprouts and hikes in Tilden Park have paid off," the *Chronicle* reported about a city health department study that found the populace far healthier than the national norm. Only 10 percent of Berkeley adults smoked—nationwide it was 25 percent. A quarter of Berkeleyans were overweight, versus half nationwide. "Berkeley residents are going to yoga classes, shopping at Berkeley Bowl," the department bragged, mentioning a grocery that regularly stocks twenty varieties of heirloom tomatoes, "they have gym memberships, they have a lot of access to recreational space and parks."[1]

But how much of this was due to the city's increasingly affluent demographics? The study also found that Berkeley's black population had a death rate double that of its white.

Berkeley, with a population of 105,385, had 57,873 Caucasians in 2005, 12,641 Asians, 8,466 Hispanics—and only 10,874 blacks. In 1980, the black population had been 20,769. Skyrocketing housing prices were blamed.

By the first decade of 2000, Berkeleyans were worrying about gentrification, a loss of character in its retail districts, the collapse of its industries, and the siege of its downtown district by scraggly, often mentally ill, homeless people. Mayor Tom Bates, a former '60s radical, found himself cracking down on "aggressive panhandling" and on people sleeping or sprawling on sidewalks.

Merchants fretted as students ignored stores in favor of Internet merchants. In 2006, when Cody's Books closed its iconic Telegraph Avenue shop, Berkeley shuddered.

On campus, people wondered how Cal could fulfill Clark Kerr's 1960 goal of educating every Californian for free, when "fees"—as they were called—kept rising.

In 2007, undergraduate fees were $4,200 a year, with total costs averaging $21,000. Undergraduate fees had gone up 90 percent in six years. Graduate students had it worse. Annual fees at the business and law schools hit $40,000. The state, which in 1965 paid for 94.4 percent of each student's education, was covering only 58 percent by 2007.

Administrators tried to make up the difference by seeking corporate and other private support. "And the question is," then-president Robert Dynes pondered, "do we end up becoming a private institution to get those resources?"[2]

And, after a statewide voter initiative in 1996 banned affirmative action, it was easy to walk across campus without spotting more than two or three black students. In 2007, only 15 percent of the freshman class was made up of "under-represented minorities"—blacks, Hispanics, and Native Americans.

The university, meanwhile, kept replacing every glade on campus with new buildings while encroaching even farther into downtown and residential neighborhoods.

Developers added to the disquietude of many by building ever taller apartment towers near campus and mixed-use projects in West Berkeley, a once low-cost area that had been home to small industries and artists.

"If we don't watch out," the *Daily Planet*'s editor, Becky O'Malley, warned, "pretty soon there'll be no Berserkeley left in Berkeley—nothing quirky, funny, artsy or even anything useful."[3]

But Berkeley still had spirit. For several years, Berkeley High School ignored a federal requirement that it provide military recruiters with information about its students. Forced to comply by threats to cut federal funding, the school allowed students to opt out. They all did—except those who ignored the request entirely. "We will not be used as tools for an unjust and imperialist war," students Krystal Elebiary and Daniel Sandoval informed the military.[4]

Meanwhile, one of the nation's top liberal blogs, the Daily Kos, was keeping the action going, thanks to its Berkeley founder Markos Moulitsas.

And in early 2008, when the city council voted to tell the U.S. Marines they were "unwelcome intruders" for running a recruiting station in town, a national furor ignited, with members of Congress threatening to defund such Berkeley institutions as the Ed Roberts Campus for disabled people and Alice Waters' "edible schoolyard" at a local school. The council vote even displeased many committed Berkeleyans, including musician Country Joe McDonald, who won fame for anti-war anthems during the Vietnam era. "It's astounding," he said of the council's initial vote. "It allows everyone to make fun of Berkeley again."[5]

The council quickly de-escalated its war with the Marines by shelving the proposed message while emphasizing Berkeley's opposition to the Iraq war.

A Berkeley "grandmother," as the press kept calling sixty-five-year-old Jane Stillwater, had already made that opposition clear. She'd made her way to Fallujah to cover the Iraqi war for her blog. Her goal was to spread a message of peace, but she was one of the tougher journalists there. "Since the invasion of Iraq was such a disaster," she asked a general, "are you going to go ahead and invade Iran?"[6]

The Berkeley BART *Plaza in the heart of downtown has often been occupied by people who are not shopping. 4-9-3-198 7048.*

Notes

So How Did Berkeley Become Berkeley?

1. *Berkeley Courier* (Berkeley, CA), September 23, 1905.
2. *Daily Californian* (Berkeley, CA), October 3, 1985, as quoted from a 1977 article from the same paper.
3. Ibid., August 26, 1985.
4. *Oakland Tribune* (Oakland, CA), July 28, 1985.
5. *Berkeley Barb* (Berkeley, CA), February 18, 1966.
6. Ibid., February 4, 1966.
7. *Tampa Tribune* (Tampa, FL), October 28, 2001.
8. *San Francisco Chronicle* (San Francisco, CA), August 31, 1986.
9. *Wall Street Journal* (New York, NY), January 11, 1989.
10. "Where We Live, Berkeley," *Contra Costa Times* (Walnut Creek, CA), special section, September 2003.
11. Tom McLaren in *Experiment and Change in Berkeley: Essays on City Politics, 1950–1975*, Institute of Governmental Studies, UC Berkeley, 1978.
12. *San Francisco Call* (San Francisco, CA), December 12, 1891.
13. *Berkeley Daily Gazette* (Berkeley, CA), May 12, 1970.
14. "Where We Live, Berkeley," *Contra Costa Times* (Walnut Creek, CA), special section, September 2003.

How Berkeley Took to the Hills

1. Joaquin Miller, "Joaquin Miller at Berkeley," *The Golden Era*, July 1886.
2. Cornelius Beach Bradley, "Walks about Berkeley," in *A Berkeley Year: A Sheaf of Nature Essays* (Berkeley: Women's Auxiliary of the First Unitarian Church, 1909). "Maraga" was Beach's spelling.
3. Agnes Edwards Partin, letters published as *Student Life at the University of California, Berkeley During and After World War I*, ed. Grace E. Moremen (Lewiston, NY: Edwin Mellen Press, 2006).
4. Campus shots by Keith seen in his Sierra paintings are in the Keith-McHenry-Pond family papers, Bancroft Library of the University of California, Berkeley.
5. "Transcript of an Interview with William E. Colby," interview by Hal Roth, Bancroft Library, 1961.
6. An undated newspaper clip in the collection, "Worth Ryder, Artist and Art Educator," Bancroft Library.

How Berkeley Remembered Its Spanish Heritage: José Domingo Peralta

1. Ina Rosenquist, "Gabriela Remembered," *Alameda County Historical Society Quarterly*, October 1998.
2. Bowman's research reported in the *Berkeley Gazette* (Berkeley, CA), August 27, 1922, and September 21, 1933; also, J. N. Bowman, "The Peraltas and Their Houses," *California Historical Society Quarterly*, September 1951. Edward Staniford wrote about the Peraltas in the *Berkeley Independent*, April 6, 1980.
3. Ina Rosenquist. "Gabriela Remembered," *Alameda County Historical Society Quarterly*, October 1998.

How Berkeley Freed Its Slaves: Napoleon Bonaparte Byrne

1. Mary Tanner Byrne, *The Byrnes of Berkeley, from letters of Mary Tanner Byrne and other sources*, Bancroft Library, 1938.
2. Marguerite C. Hussey, *The Byrne Family and Life in Northeast Berkeley during the 1890s*, ed. Karen Jorgensen Esmaili, Berkeley History Project, Bancroft Library, 1982.
3. Mary Tanner Byrne, *The Byrnes of Berkeley, from letters of Mary Tanner Byrne and other sources*, Bancroft Library, 1938.

How Berkeley Founded a University

1. Durant's tale is based on a lost interview, told in Millicent W. Shinn, "The University of California," *Overland Monthly*, October–December 1892; William Carey Jones, *The Illustrated History of the University of California* (Berkeley: Students Cooperative Society, 1901).
2. William Carey Jones, *The Illustrated History of the University of California* (Berkeley: Students Cooperative Society, 1901).
3. Millicent W. Shinn, "The University of California," *Overland Monthly*, October–December 1892.

How Berkeley Developed a Cow Town

1. Wilhemine F. Bolsted Cianciarulo, "Berkeley as I Knew it in the Early Years," typescript in the Swingle Collection of the Berkeley Public Library History Room.

How University Students Got the Spirit

1. *Register of the University of California*, 1877–78.
2. Ibid.
3. John Muir, "Reminiscences of Joseph Le Conte," in the *Joseph Le Conte Memorials*, Bancroft Library.
4. *Occident* (Berkeley, CA), a student magazine, February 1882.
5. Blue and Gold student yearbook, 1873–74.

6. *The Berkeley Advocate* (Berkeley, CA), January 23, 1879.
7. *Occident* (Berkeley, CA), November 17, 1882.
8. Ibid., May 4, 1882.

How Berkeley's Coeds Doffed Their Hats

1. Lilian Bridgman, *The Lilian Bridgman Papers, 1881–1977*. Bancroft Library.
2. *Berkeley Courier* (Berkeley, CA), October 29, 1904.
3. Ibid., January 28, 1905.
4. Ibid., March 15, 1905.
5. Ibid., August 19, 1905.

How Berkeley Communicated by Sign: The School for the Deaf and Blind

1. Leon Richardson, "Berkeley Culture, University of California, Highlights and University Extension, 1892–1960," oral history by Amelia R. Fry, Bancroft Library, 1962.
2. William Caldwell, Wilkinson's obituary in *California News* (Berkeley, CA), (the school publication), April 1918.
3. *San Francisco Examiner* (San Francisco, CA), June 13, 1900.
4. *The Educator* (Pennsylvania State University), March 1895.
5. *Berkeley Daily Gazette* (Berkeley, CA), April 1, 1925.
6. Tilden obituary, *San Francisco Chronicle* (San Francisco, CA), August 7, 1935. "Mallet and chisel" from an unidentified obituary in the Douglas Tilden file of the Berkeley Public Library History Room.

How Berkeley Entertained a Great Resort: M. B. Curtis

1. William Warren Ferrier, *Berkeley California: The Story of the Evolution of a Hamlet into a City of Culture and Commerce* (Berkeley: Sather Gate Bookstore, 1933).
2. *Berkeley Independent* (Berkeley, CA), May 15, 1911.

3. Theater profile, *New York Times* (New York, NY), December 12, 1885.

4. Edmond M. Gagey, *The San Francisco Stage: A History* (New York: Columbia University Press, 1950).

5. Review, *Los Angeles Times* (Los Angeles, CA), June 12, 1886; also June 9 on page 2, an advertisement for the play.

6. Hal Johnson column, *Berkeley Gazette* (Berkeley, CA), 1950s (undated clip, Berkeley Public Library History Room).

7. *Oakland Tribune* (Oakland, CA), December 29, 1920.

8. Pete Fanning, *Great Crimes of the West* (San Francisco: Ed Barry Co., 1929).

9. Accounts of the trial, *San Francisco Call* (San Francisco, CA), September 12 and 16, 1891, October 11, 1891; January 12, February 4 and 26, and November 15, 1892.

10. Obituary, *Los Angeles Times* (Los Angeles, CA), December 30, 1920.

How Berkeley Got Religion

1. Helen Benedict, "The Bay Area's Holy Hill," *Berkeley Independent* and *Gazette* (Berkeley, CA), September 11, 1980.

2. *San Francisco Chronicle* (San Francisco, CA), February 1, 1993.

3. "In memoriam, William Frederic Badè, 1871–1936," *Bulletin of Pacific School of Religion*, June 1936.

4. Ibid.

5. *Berkeley Daily Gazette* (Berkeley, CA), September 21, 1926.

6. Ibid.

How Berkeley Became Bohemian

1. *Occident* (Berkeley, CA), October 6, 1881.

2. Eugen Neuhaus, *William Keith, the Man and the Artist* (San Francisco, 1938).

3. Charles Keeler, *Charles Augustus Keeler Papers*, Bancroft Library of the University of California.

4. "Mme. Pensée," *Berkeley Courier* (Berkeley, CA), July 7, 1906.

5. Ibid.

6. *Berkeley Courier* (Berkeley, CA), February 4, 1905.

7. *Berkeley Independent* (Berkeley, CA), October 30, 1912.

How Berkeley Donned Tunics: Florence Treadwell Boynton

1. *Dance at the Temple of the Wings, the Boynton-Quitzow family in Berkeley: oral history transcript and related material, 1972–1973*, Bancroft Library.

2. Jacomena Maybeck, *Maybeck: The Family View* (Berkeley: Berkeley Architectural Heritage Association, 1980).

How Berkeley Revealed Nature's Spirit: William Keith

1. Eugen Neuhaus. *William Keith, the Man and the Artist* (San Francisco, 1938).

2. Ibid.

3. Charles Keeler letter of July 14, 1892, from the *Charles Augustus Keeler Papers*, Bancroft Library.

4. Muir letter in the *Keith-McHenry-Pond Family Papers, 1841–1961*, Bancroft Library.

5. Emily P. B. Hay, *William Keith as Prophet Painter* (San Francisco: Paul Elder, 1916).

6. Charles Keeler, "The American Turner," *Sunshine*, May 1898.

7. *Berkeley Daily Gazette* (Berkeley, CA), May 20, 1896.

How Berkeley Promoted the Good Life: Charles Keeler

1. Keeler letter, in *Charles Augustus Keeler Papers*, Bancroft, Library, September 5, 1929.

2. On Hard Times in New York, letters 1914–1926 in Keeler Papers.

3. On Cosmic Society, letters and pamphlets in Keeler Papers.

4. Charles Keeler, *An Epitome of Cosmic Religion* (Berkeley: At the Sign of the Live Oak, 1925).

How Berkeley Developed Its Look: Bernard Maybeck

1. Winthrop Sargeant, typescript for his 1949 book, *Geniuses, Goddesses and People*, in *Bernard Maybeck clippings and scrapbook*, UC Berkeley Environmental Design Library.

2. Jacomena Maybeck, *Maybeck: The Family View* (Berkeley: Berkeley Architectural Heritage Association, 1980).

How Berkeley's University Cultivated a Beautiful Campus

1. William Carey Jones, *Illustrated History of the University of California* (Berkeley: Students' Cooperative Society, 1901).

2. Ibid.

3. William Warren Ferrier, *Berkeley California: The Story of the Evolution of a Hamlet into a City of Culture and Commerce* (Berkeley: self-published), 1933.

4. Ibid.

How Berkeley Founded National Parks

1. Frank Soulé, "Joe Le Conte in the Sierra," *Sierra Club Bulletin*, January 1902.

2. Charles Keeler, letter of June 7, 1892, in *Charles Augustus Keeler Papers*, Bancroft Library.

3. Bonnie Johanna Gisel, *Kindred and Related Spirits: The Letters of John Muir and Jeanne C. Carr* (Salt Lake City: University of Utah Press, 2001).

4. Rod Miller, *John Muir: Magnificent Tramp* (New York: Forge, 2005).

5. William E. Colby. *Transcript of an Interview with William E. Colby*, Bancroft Library.

6. Ibid.

7. S. B. Christy, profile of Muir, *Bulletin of the Department of Mining and Metallurgy*, 1902.

8. Joseph Le Conte, *Correspondence 1858–1900* in *Le Conte Family Papers*, Bancroft Library.

9. Frank Soulé, "Joe Le Conte in the Sierra," *Sierra Club Bulletin*, January 1902.

10. William E. Colby, *Transcript of an Interview with William E. Colby*, Bancroft Library.

How Berkeley Became Asian

1. *Berkeley Advocate* (Berkeley, CA), February 9, 1878.

2. Advertisement, *Berkeley Advocate* (Berkeley, CA), April 13, 1878.

3. *Berkeley Advocate* (Berkeley, CA), April 27, 1878.

4. *Berkeley Courier* (Berkeley, CA), January 14, 1905.

5. John Naoki Fujii, *Fujii* (Berkeley: self-published, 1986). A family history, Bancroft Library.

6. *Berkeley Daily Gazette* (Berkeley, CA), June 17, 1903.

7. *Berkeley Courier* (Berkeley, CA), June 10, 1905.

8. Ibid., August 4, 1906.

How Berkeley Created a Great University

1. *Occident* (Berkeley, CA), February 9, 1882.

2. Millicent Washburn Shinn, *The University of California*. (San Francisco: Overland Monthly, 1892). Reprints of her articles from *Overland Monthly*, Bancroft Library.

3. *Berkeley Daily Gazette* (Berkeley, CA), July 14, 1954.

4. *Berkeley Courier* (Berkeley, CA), May 5, 1926.

5. Benjamin Ide Wheeler, *The Abundant Life* (Berkeley: University of California Press, 1926).

How Berkeley Went Dry

1. Dorcas James Spencer, *A History of the Woman's Christian Temperance Union of Northern and Central California*, (Oakland: West Coast Printing Co., 1920).
2. *Berkeley Courier* (Berkeley, CA), July 29, 1905.
3. *Berkeley Advocate* (Berkeley, CA), advertisement that ran daily throughout 1879.
4. *Berkeley Independent* (Berkeley, CA), February 12, 1913.
5. Ibid., November 2, 1912.
6. *Berkeley Courier* (Berkeley, CA), September 23, 1905.
7. Ibid., October 28, 1905.
8. Ibid., August 25, 1906.

How Berkeley Boomed

1. *Berkeley Courier* (Berkeley, CA), February 24, 1906.
2. Ibid., September 9, 1905.
3. Ibid., September 2, 1905.
4. Ibid., September 16, 1905.
5. Ibid., April 7, 1906.
6. *Berkeley Courier* (Berkeley, CA), September 16, 1905.
7. *Berkeley Courier* (Berkeley, CA), March 10, 1906.
8. Mason-McDuffie Co., *Claremont: A Private Residence Park at Berkeley*, promotional pamphlet, Berkeley Architectural Heritage Association collection, circa 1908.

How Berkeley Pioneered Modern Crime Fighting

1. *Berkeley Daily Gazette* (Berkeley, CA), November 18, 1903.
2. *Berkeley Courier* (Berkeley, CA), January 28, 1905.
3. Ibid., June 10, 1905.
4. Ibid., August 12, 1905.
5. *Berkeley Daily Gazette* (Berkeley, CA), September 21, 1929, and April 29, 1930.
6. Unidentified newspaper clipping, 1920s, August Vollmer file, Berkeley Public Library History Room.

7. *Berkeley Daily Gazette* (Berkeley, CA), April 29, 1930.
8. Eloise Keeler, *Eloise Keeler Papers, circa 1938–1986*, Bancroft Library. The story of Chickie is from a typescript in the papers, *My Brother Leonarde and His Lie-Detector*.
9. *Colliers* (New York, NY), November 8, 1924.
10. Obituary, *Los Angeles Times* (Los Angeles, CA), November 5, 1955.

How Berkeley Pioneered Women's Rights

1. *Berkeley Daily Gazette* (Berkeley, CA), May 20, 1896.
2. Business card in *Keith-McHenry Pond Family Papers*, Bancroft Library.
3. *Berkeley Daily Gazette* (Berkeley, CA), May 20, 1896.
4. Ibid., January 18, 1902.
5. *Berkeley Courier* (Berkeley, CA), February 11, 1905.

How Berkeley Trod the Boards: Sam Hume

1. UC Class of 1908 program in *Samuel J. and Portia Bell Hume Papers*, Bancroft Library.
2. Flyer in the Theater File, Berkeley Historical Society.
3. Eugene O'Neill, September 1940 letter in *The Berkeley Playmakers: scrapbook, 1924–1948*, Bancroft Library.
4. *Boston Evening Transcript* (Boston, MA), June 18, 1925.
5. Hume letters in *Samuel J. and Portia Bell Hume Papers*, Bancroft Library.
6. *Marysville Appeal-Democrat* (Marysville, CA), January 10, 1929, in Hume papers.
7. Unidentified newspaper clip in Hume papers, November 26, 1928.
8. Hume letters in *Samuel J. and Portia Bell Hume Papers*, Bancroft Library.
9. Ibid.

How Berkeley Went Socialist: Mayor J. Stitt Wilson

1. *Berkeley Daily Gazette* (Berkeley, CA), March 14, 1911.
2. Ibid., March 22, 1911.
3. Ibid., March 29, 1911.
4. *Berkeley Courier* (Berkeley, CA), January 14, 1905.
5. J. Stitt Wilson, *The Barbary Coast in a Barbarous Land: Or the Harlots and the Pharisees* (Los Angeles: Socialist Party of America, 1913), Bancroft Library.
6. *Berkeley Daily Gazette,* (Berkeley, CA), June 8, 1911.
7. *Berkeley Independent* (Berkeley, CA), October 7, 1912.
8. Ibid., January 21, 1913.
9. Ibid., November 2, 1912.

How Berkeley Caught the Flu

1. Agnes Edwards Partin, ed. Grace E Moreman. *Student Life at the University of California, Berkeley During and After World War I, the Letters Of Agnes Edwards Partin, 1917–1921* (Lewiston, New York: Edwin Mellen Press, 2006).
2. Eugen Neuhaus, *Reminiscences: Bay Area Art and the University of California Art Department: Oral History Transcript.* Conducted by Suzanne B. Riess for the Regional Cultural History Project, University of California, Berkeley, 1961. Bancroft Library.

How Berkeley Burned

1. *San Francisco Chronicle* (San Francisco, CA), September 18, 1923.
2. Aubrey Boyd, *Berkeley Fire 1923* (Berkeley: George E. Russell Aero-Photographer, and the Camera Shop, 1923).
3. *Dance at the Temple of the Wings, the Boynton-Quitzow family in Berkeley: oral history transcript and related material, 1972–1973.* Conducted 1972 by Suzanne Riess and Margaretta Mitchell for the Regional Oral History Office, Bancroft Library, University of California, Berkeley.
4. *Berkeley Daily Gazette* (Berkeley, CA), September 18, 1923.
5. *San Francisco Chronicle* (San Francisco, CA), September 20, 1923.
6. Ibid.
7. Ibid.
8. Ibid.
9. Ibid.
10. *Dance at the Temple of the Wings, the Boynton-Quitzow family in Berkeley: oral history transcript and related material, 1972–1973.* Conducted 1972 by Suzanne Riess and Margaretta Mitchell for the Regional Oral History Office, Bancroft Library, University of California, Berkeley.
11. *San Francisco Chronicle* (San Francisco, CA), September 20, 1923.

How Berkeley Won the Big Game

1. *Berkeley Advocate* (Berkeley, CA), January 12, 1878.
2. *Daily Californian* (Berkeley, CA), April 13, 14, 17, and 18, 1899.
3. *Berkeley Daily Gazette* (Berkeley, CA), October 23, 1922.
4. Benjamin Ide Wheeler, "Shall football be ended or mended?" *American Monthly Review of Reviews*, January 1906.
5. *Daily Californian* (Berkeley, CA), October 27, 1922.
6. Brick Morse, *California Football History* (Berkeley: Gillick Press, 1937).
7. *Daily Californian* (Berkeley, CA), November 24, 1922.
8. Ibid., November 27, 1922.
9. Ibid., January 18, 1926.

How Berkeley Spurned Spanking

1. George Petitt, "Berkeley in the Good Old Days," in *Experiment and Change in Berkeley: Essays on City Politics 1950–1975* (Berkeley: Institute of Governmental Studies, 1978).
2. City of Berkeley, *Seventh Annual Report of the Mayor*, 1916.
3. City of Berkeley, *Annual Report of the Mayor*, 1935.
4. *Berkeley Daily Gazette* (Berkeley, CA), February 21, 1919.
5. Mayor's report, 1927.
6. Clip files from Berkeley Public Health Department in Institute of Government Studies. Pamphlets, reports, news clipping.
7. Ibid.
8. *Oakland Tribune* (Oakland, CA), April 26, 1923.
9. Ibid.
10. *San Francisco Chronicle* (San Francisco, CA), July 18, 2007.

How Berkeley Invented Regional Parks

1. *Berkeley Daily Gazette* (Berkeley, CA), April 16, 21, 23, 24, 27, 28, and 30, 1908.
2. Unidentified newspaper clip in East Bay Regional Park District Archive scrapbooks.
3. *Stockton Record*, April 25, 1931.
4. *Berkeley Daily Gazette* (Berkeley, CA), March 19, 1931.
5. Ibid., November 8, 1934.

How Berkeley's Howled for Sproul

1. *Berkeley Courier* (Berkeley, CA), May 16, 1931.
2. Unidentified news clip from 1936 in the Robert Gordon Sproul file at the Berkeley Public Library History Room.
3. *New York Times* (New York, NY), September 12, 1975
4. Will Connolly, "Will Connolly Says" column, *San Francisco Chronicle* (San Francisco, CA), March 12, 1939.
5. *Berkeley Daily Gazette* (Berkeley, CA), March 10, 1939.
6. Ibid.
7. Ibid.

How Berkeley Cooperated

1. Paul Rauber, Profile of the Berkeley Co-op, *East Bay Express*, (Berkeley, CA), June 17, 1988.
2. Berkeley Historical Society, *A Conversation with Robert Neptune*, conducted in 1987 (Berkeley: Berkeley Historical Society, 1996).
3. Lee Gomes, undated article in the *Oakland Tribune* (Oakland, CA), in the Berkeley Co-op file at the Berkeley Public Library History Room.
4. Berkeley Co-op pamphlets and flyers and newsletters, in the Berkeley Co-op file at the Berkeley Public Library History Room.
5. William Brand, "Can the Co-op Be Saved?" *East Bay Express* (Berkeley, CA), January 22, 1982.
6. *Los Angeles Times* (Los Angeles, CA), March 8, 1984.
7. William Brand, "Can the Co-op Be Saved?" *East Bay Express* (Berkeley, CA), January 22, 1982.
8. Lee Gomes, undated article in the *Oakland Tribune* (Oakland, CA), in the Berkeley Co-op file at the Berkeley Public Library History Room.

How Berkeley Fought World War II

1. *Berkeley Daily Gazette* (Berkeley, CA), December 8, 1941.
2. Undated 1943 clip from the *Berkeley Daily Gazette* (Berkeley, CA), in the World War II file at the Berkeley Public Library History Room.
3. *Berkeley Daily Gazette* (Berkeley, CA), June 16, 1942.
4. Ibid., May 22, 1943.
5. Ibid., March 10, 1942.
6. Ibid., September 17, 28, and 29, 1942.
7. Ibid., February 1 and 17, 1944, and May 9, 1945.
8. *Berkeley War Effort*, November 16, 1942. Pamphlet in the World War II file at the Berkeley Public Library History Room.

9. *Berkeley Daily Gazette* (Berkeley, CA), December 20, 1944, January 1, 2, and 29, 1945, and October 3, 1945.

10. Ibid., June 6 and 29, 1942; September 28, 1942; August 17, 19, and 20, 1943.

11. Ibid., August 18, 1943.

How Berkeley's Japanese Persevered through Adversity

1. *Daily Californian* (Berkeley, CA), February 18, 1986.

2. Yoshiko Uchida, *Desert Exile: The Uprooting of a Japanese-American Family* (Seattle: University of Washington Press, 1984).

3. *Daily Californian* (Berkeley, CA), February 18, 1986.

4. Robert Yamada, *The Japanese American Experience: The Berkeley Legacy* (Berkeley: Berkeley Historical Society, 1995).

5. *Daily Californian* (Berkeley, CA), October 19, 1976.

6. Letters between Frank Kawahara and Mrs. Smith in the World War II files of the Berkeley Public Library History Room.

7. Robert Yamada, *The Japanese American Experience: The Berkeley Legacy* (Berkeley: The Berkeley Historical Society, 1995).

8. John Naoki Fujii, *Fujii* (Berkeley: self-published, 1986). A family history. Bancroft Library.

How Berkeley Invented the Bomb

1. *Daily Californian* (Berkeley, CA), August 10, 2001.

2. Gregg Herken, *Brotherhood of the Bomb: The Tangled Lives and Loyalties of Robert Oppenheimer, Ernest Lawrence, and Edward Teller* (New York: Henry Holt, 2002).

3. Margaret Talbot, "Days after Trinity," *East Bay Express* (Berkeley, CA), March 23, 1984.

4. *Berkeley Daily Gazette* (Berkeley, CA), August 28, 1945.

How Berkeley Invented Listener-Sponsored Radio

1. Bernard Taper, "A Radio Experiment Signs Off the Air," *San Francisco Chronicle* (San Francisco, CA), August 13, 1950.

2. KPFA Folio, November 1971, in KPFA file, Berkeley Public Library History Room.

3. *Barron's* (Boston, MA.), April 6, 1970.

4. Ibid.

5. Obituary, *San Francisco Chronicle* (San Francisco, CA), August 2, 1957.

6. *New York Times* (New York, NY), July 23, 1999.

How Berkeley Swore an Oath

1. Conversation with Robert Royston, November 24, 2006.

2. *Group for Academic Freedom records, 1950–1956*, University of California, Berkeley, Bancroft Library.

3. Committee on Academic Freedom of the Academic Senate, *The Consequences of the Abrogation of Tenure*, a report, Bancroft Library, February 1, 1951.

4. *San Francisco Call* (San Francisco, CA), June 8, 1951.

How Berkeley Broke the Racial Barrier

1. Bill Wyman, "Roots: The Origins of Black Politics," *East Bay Express* (Berkeley, CA), August 7, 1987.

2. Agnes Edwards Partin, ed. Grace E. Moreman, *Student Life at the University of California, Berkeley During and After World War I, the Letters of Agnes Edwards Partin, 1917–1921* (Lewiston, New York: Edwin Mellen Press, 2006).

3. Bill Wyman, "Roots: The Origins of Black Politics," *East Bay Express* (Berkeley, CA), August 7, 1987.

4. Ibid.

5. Ruth Acty, *Ruth Acty: First African American Teacher in the Berkeley Unified School District* (Berkeley: Berkeley Historical Society, 2001).

6. Obituary for Rumford, *Oakland Tribune* (Oakland, CA), June 13, 1986.

7. "Meet Wilmont Sweeny," *Berkeley Daily Gazette* (Berkeley, CA), August 18, 1961.

8. *Berkeley Daily Gazette* (Berkeley, CA), June 25, 1971.

9. Ibid., July 22, 1971.

10. *Oakland Tribune* (Oakland, CA), February 19, 1989.

How Berkeley Pioneered School Integration

1. Berkeley Unified School District (BUSD), Integration Progress Report, April 26, 1968.

2. Robert Coles, with photographs by Peter T. Whitney and Carol Baldwin, *The Buses Roll* (New York: Norton, 1974).

3. Howard Maves, BUSD report, September 1968.

4. BUSD Progress Report, June 1963.

5. *Berkeley Daily Gazette* (Berkeley, CA), July 30, 1959.

6. Ibid., June 5, 1964.

7. Carol Sibley, *Building community trust, Berkeley school integration and other civic endeavors, 1943–1978, oral history transcript.* Interview conducted by Eleanor Glaser and Gabrielle Morris in 1978. Regional Oral History Office, UC Berkeley, Bancroft Library.

8. *Berkeley Daily Gazette* (Berkeley, CA), May 20, 1964.

9. BUSD board minutes, December 5, 1967.

10. Sally E. James, *School Desegregation in Berkeley, California: A Staff Report of the U.S. Commission on Civil Rights* (Washington, D.C., 1977).

11. Editorial, *Berkeley Daily Gazette* (Berkeley, CA), October 9, 1967.

12. Norene Harris, *The Integration of American Schools: Problems, Experiences, Solutions* (Boston: Allyn and Bacon, 1975).

13. BUSD board minutes, October 1, 1968.

How Berkeley Promoted Free Speech

1. Ilona Hancock, " 'New Politics' in Berkeley: A Personal View," in *Experiment and Change in Berkeley: Essays on City Politics, 1950–1975* (Berkeley: Institute of Governmental Studies, 1978).

2. Steven Warshaw, *The Trouble in Berkeley* (Berkeley: Diablo Press, 1965).

3. *San Francisco Examiner* (San Francisco, CA), October 1, 1964.

4. Steve Rubenstein, *Cal Finally Embraces Lefties—with Lattes* (San Francisco-Chronicle, 1998).

5. Steven Warshaw, *The Trouble in Berkeley* (Berkeley: Diablo Press, 1965).

How Berkeley Rescued the Bay

1. *Save San Francisco Bay Association, 1961–1986*, oral history transcript, Regional Oral History Office of the University of California, Bancroft Library. Interviews conducted by Malca Chall.

2. City of Berkeley, Annual Report, 1916–1917.

3. City of Berkeley, Annual Report, 1925–1926.

4. *Oakland Tribune* (Oakland, CA), July 31, 1929.

5. City of Berkeley, Annual Report, 1949. In the collection of the Berkeley Architectural Heritage Association.

6. Harold Gilliam, introduction to *Save San Francisco Bay Association, 1961–1986*, oral history transcript, Regional Oral History Office of the University of California, Bancroft Library. Interviews conducted by Malca Chall.

7. Sylvia McLaughlin, in *Save San Francisco Bay* oral history.

8. Ibid.

9. Harold Gilliam, *San Francisco Chronicle* (San Francisco, CA), April 22, 2007.
10. Ibid.

How Berkeley Preserved Its Neighborhoods

1. George Pettitt, "Berkeley in the good old days," in *Experiment and Change in Berkeley: Essays on City Politics 1950–1975* (Berkeley: Institute of Governmental Studies, 1978).
2. John Kenyon, "One Man's Berkeley," *East Bay Monthly* (Berkeley, CA), August 1983.
3. Conte Seely and Jon Sullivan, *Berkeley One and Only* (Berkeley: Command Performance Press, 2006).
4. *San Francisco Chronicle* (San Francisco, CA), February 22, 2004.
5. Martin Snapp, "Who was Joseph Charles?" *Contra Costa Times* (Walnut Creek, CA), March 22, 2002.

How Berkeley Became the People's Republic

1. Tracy Johnson, article on recall of D'Armey Bailey, *San Francisco Magazine* (San Francisco, CA), August 1973.
2. Conversation with author, September 2007.
3. Ilona Hancock, "New Politics in Berkeley: A Personal View," in *Experiment and Change in Berkeley: Essays on City Politics, 1950–1975* (Berkeley: Institute of Governmental Studies, 1978).
4. *Berkeley Daily Gazette* (Berkeley, CA), February 26, 1973.
5. John K. DeBonis, *Quotations from Chairman John K. DeBonis*. Pamphlet, late 1960s (Berkeley: unknown publisher). In John DeBonis file, Berkeley Public Library History Room.
6. William Moore, "Foe of radicals takes a new look at Berkeley," *San Francisco Chronicle* (San Francisco, CA), May 3, 1971.
7. *Berkeley Daily Gazette* (Berkeley, CA), April 5, 1961.

8. Joseph Lyford, *The Berkeley Archipelago* (Chicago: Regnery Gateway, 1982).
9. Thomas McLaren, in *Experiment and Change in Berkeley: Essays on City Politics 1950–1975* (Berkeley: Institute of Governmental Studies, 1978).
10. Tracy Johnson, article on recall of D'Armey Bailey, *San Francisco Magazine* (San Francisco, CA), August 1973.
11. *Tribune* (Oakland, CA), August 14, 2004.
12. Political flyer, D'Armey Bailey file, Berkeley Public Library History Room.
13. *Berkeley Daily Gazette* (Berkeley, CA), August 17, 1973.
14. Thomas McLaren, in *Experiment and Change in Berkeley: Essays on City Politics 1950–1975* (Berkeley: Institute of Governmental Studies, 1978).
15. Ilona Hancock, "New Politics in Berkeley: A Personal View," in *Experiment and Change in Berkeley: Essays on City Politics, 1950–1975* (Berkeley: Institute of Governmental Studies, 1978).

How Berkeley Erupted

1. John K. DeBonis, *Quotations from Chairman John K. DeBonis*. Pamphlet, late 1960s (Berkeley: unknown publisher). In John DeBonis file, Berkeley Public Library History Room.
2. *San Francisco Examiner* (San Francisco, CA), August 13, 1965.
3. *San Francisco Chronicle* (San Francisco, CA), February 12, 2008.
4. *Berkeley Daily Gazette* (Berkeley, CA), April 16, 1970.
5. *Oakland Tribune* (Oakland, CA), April 17, 1970.
6. *Berkeley Daily Gazette* (Berkeley, CA), April 16, 1970.
7. Ibid., February 14, 1969.
8. Ibid., February 22, 1969.
9. Ibid., February 6, 1969.

How Berkeley Went "Berserkeley"

1. Joel Selvin, *San Francisco Chronicle* (San Francisco, CA), July 12, 2007.
2. Thomas Farber, *Tales for the Son of My Unborn Child* (New York: Dutton, 1975).
3. Del Rainer, *One World Family Commune, My Story.* On the Web site Galactic Messenger Network, www.galactic messenger.com.
4. *Berkeley Barb* (Berkeley, CA), September 30, 1966; "Watusi," *Berkeley Barb*, February 18, 1966.
5. Ibid., February 4, 1966.
6. Ibid., January 13, 1967.
7. Ibid., January 27, 1968.

How Berkeley's Telegraph Avenue Suffered

1. Pat and Fred Cody, "A View from the Avenue," in *Experiment and Change in Berkeley: Essays on City Politics 1950–1975* (Berkeley: Institute of Governmental Studies, 1978).
2. Ibid.
3. Ibid.
4. Ibid.

How Berkeley Battled for a Park

1. John Kenyon, "One Man's Berkeley," *East Bay Monthly* (Berkeley, CA), August 1983.
2. Stewart Albert, *Berkeley Barb* (Berkeley, CA), May 23, 1969.
3. *San Francisco Chronicle* (San Francisco, CA), June 26, 2007.
4. Wallace Johnson, "Berkeley: Twelve Years as the Nation in Microcosm," in *Experiment and Change in Berkeley: Essays on City Politics 1950–1975* (Berkeley: Institute of Governmental Studies, 1978).
5. Ibid.
6. Joe Pichirallo, *Daily Californian* (Berkeley, CA), May 16, 1969.
7. *Daily Californian* (Berkeley, CA), May 21, 1969.
8. Rick Heid, *Berkeley Barb* (Berkeley, CA), May 23, 1969.

How Berkeley Got Good Taste

1. Writers Program, *Berkeley: The First Seventy-Five Years* (Berkeley: Gillick Press, 1941). Quotes Juan Crespi's diary.
2. *Berkeley Courier* (Berkeley, CA), advertisements, October 8 and November 26, 1904; July 5 and December 3, 1905.
3. Editorial, *Berkeley Courier* (Berkeley, CA), August 18, 1906.
4. David Darlington, "The Stimulating World of Mr. Peet," *East Bay Express* (Berkeley, CA), July 13, 1984.
5. Vicky Elliott, "Mr. Peet," *East Bay Monthly* (Berkeley, CA), October 2000.
6. David Darlington, "The Stimulating World of Mr. Peet," *East Bay Express* (Berkeley, CA), July 13, 1984.
7. Cheese Board Collective, *The Cheese Board: Collective Works: Bread, Pastry, Cheese, Pizza* (Berkeley: Ten Speed Press, 2003).
8. Ibid.
9. *Oakland Tribune* (Oakland, CA), August 21, 1991.
10. *San Francisco Chronicle* (San Francisco, CA), August 21, 1991.
11. Ruth Stein, *San Francisco Chronicle* (San Francisco, CA), December 10, 1975.
12. Stan Sesser, *San Francisco Examiner* (San Francisco, CA), June 10, 1983.

How Berkeley Invented the Hot Tub

1. Marton Dunai, Profile of Jacuzzi Family, *West County Times* (Richmond, CA), April 7, 2007.
2. "Keeping Fit in California," *New York Times*, January 8, 1978.

How Berkeley Found Its Sound

1. Blue and Gold student yearbook, 1886.
2. Derk Richardson, *Bay Guardian* (San Francisco, CA), October 1991.
3. *East Bay Express* (Berkeley, CA), June 18, 1993.
4. Ibid.

How Berkeley Discovered Yuppies

1. Alice Kahn, "Yuppie!" *East Bay Express* (Berkeley, CA), June 10, 1983.
2. Kahn's home page on the Web site for Kaiser Permanente, www.permanente.net/home page.

How Berkeley Invented Disability Rights

1. *Daily Californian* (Berkeley, CA), April 25, 1997.
2. Roberts's obituary, *San Francisco Chronicle* (San Francisco, CA), May 15, 1999.
3. Burr Snider, "Up and Fighting for the Rights of Disabled," *San Francisco Examiner* (San Francisco, CA), February 13, 1983.
4. Ibid.
5. *Berkeley Gazette* (Berkeley, CA), October 28, 1975.
6. Linda B. Joffee, "A Different Way of Touching," *California Living* (magazine of the *Sunday Examiner-Chronicle*) (San Francisco, CA), July 23, 1978.
7. Sonny Kleinfield, "Declaring Independence in Berkeley," *Psychology Today*, August 1979.
8. Ibid.
9. Ibid.

How Berkeley Women Turned Uppity

1. Lisa Gerrard, "Yours in Sisterhood," *The Berkeley Literary Women's Revolution: Essays from Marsha's Salon* (Jefferson, NC: McFarland and Co., 2005).
2. Ibid.
3. Ibid.
4. Ibid.
5. Flyer in the Women's Liberation File, Berkeley Public Library History Room.
6. *The Berkeley Literary Women's Revolution: Essays from Marsha's Salon* (Jefferson, NC: McFarland and Co., 2005).

How Berkeley's Gays Held Hands

1. Mike McGrath, "Gay Politics the East Bay Way," *East Bay Express* (Berkeley, CA), June 24, 1983.
2. Dinitia Smith, *New York Times* (New York, NY), October 17, 2005.
3. Paul Christensen, "Robert Duncan's Life and Career." On the Web site of the Department of English, University of Illinois, Urbana-Champaign, www.english.uiuc.edu/maps /poets/a_f/duncan/life.htm.
4. *Daily Californian* (Berkeley, CA), July 11, 1995.
5. *Oakland Tribune* (Oakland, CA), October 9, 1987.
6. Ibid., November 16, 1997.
7. Linnea Due, "Loud and Queer," *East Bay Express* (Berkeley, CA), February 15, 1991.

How Berkeley Indians Rallied 'Round Their Sacred Ground

1. Wilhemine F. Bolsted Cianciarulo, "Berkeley as I Knew It in the Early Years," typescript in the Swingle Collection of the Berkeley Public Library History Room.
2. Nels Nelson, *Excavation of the Emeryville Shellmound* (Berkeley: Archeological Research facility, reprinted 1996).
3. *Berkeley Voice* (Berkeley, CA), July 30, 1999.
4. *Daily Californian* (Berkeley, CA), September 18, 2007.
5. *San Francisco Chronicle* (San Francisco, CA), January 7, 2007, and March 18, 2007.

6. *San Francisco Chronicle* (San Francisco, CA), September 1, 2007.

How Berkeley Turned Green

1. Richard Brenneman, *Daily Planet* (Berkeley, CA), July 29, 2005.
2. *California Magazine* (San Francisco, CA), September 2006.
3. *San Francisco Chronicle* (San Francisco, CA), May 24, 2007.
4. Ibid., March 5, 2007.
5. Ibid., May 23, 2007.
6. Ibid., October 5, 2007.
7. *California Magazine* (San Francisco, CA), September 2007.

How Berkeley Worried

1. *San Francisco Chronicle* (San Francisco, CA), May 23, 2007.
2. *Contra Costa Times* (Walnut Creek, CA), October 8, 2007.
3. Becky O'Malley, "Keeping the Berserkeley in Berkeley," *Berkeley Daily Planet*, August 2007.
4. *San Francisco Chronicle* (San Francisco, CA), June 12, 2007.
5. Ibid., February 12, 2008.
6. *Contra Costa Times* (Walnut Creek, CA), September 30, 2007.

Bibliography

Berkeley Architectural Heritage Association. www.berkeleyheritage.com. Many articles on the city's history and heritage by Daniella Thompson, Anthony Bruce, and other contributors.

Berkeley Historical Society. *A History of Berkeley*. Berkeley: Berkeley Historical Society, 1978.

———. *Looking Back at Berkeley: A Pictorial History of a Diverse City*." Berkeley: Berkeley Historical Society, 1984.

Berkeley Writers Program. *Berkeley: The First Seventy-Five Years*. Berkeley: Gillick Press, 1941.

Bowman, J. N. "The Peraltas and Their Houses." *California Historical Society Quarterly* (September 1951).

Boyd, Aubrey. *Berkeley Fire 1923*. Berkeley: George E. Russell Aero-Photographer, and the Camera Shop, 1923.

Boynton-Quitzow Family. *Dance at the Temple of the Wings, the Boynton-Quitzow Family in Berkeley: Oral History Transcript and Related Material, 1972–1973*. Conducted 1972 by Suzanne Riess and Margaretta Mitchell for the Regional Oral History Office, Bancroft Library, University of California, Berkeley.

Bridgman, Lilian. Papers, 1881–1977. Bancroft Library Papers, University of California, Berkeley.

Byrne family. Papers, 1858–1935. Bancroft Library, University of California, Berkeley.

Byrne, Mary Tanner. "The Byrnes of Berkeley. From letters of Mary Tanner Byrne and other sources." *California Historical Society Quarterly*. San Francisco, 1938.

Cardwell, Kenneth. *Bernard Maybeck: Artisan, Architect, Artist*. Santa Barbara: Peregrine Smith, 1977.

Cerny, Susan Dinkelspiel. *Berkeley Landmarks*. Berkeley: Berkeley Architectural Heritage Association, 2001.

Chester, Jonathan and Dave Weinstein. *Berkeley Rocks: Building with Nature*. Berkeley: Ten Speed Press, 2006.

Cianciarulo, Wilhelmine F. Bolsted. *Berkeley as I Knew It in the Early Years.* Typescript in the Swingle Collection of the Berkeley Public Library History Room.

Colby, William E. Transcript of an interview with William E. Colby. Conducted by Hal Roth, Bancroft Library, University of California, Berkeley.

Crouchett, Lawrence P. *William Byron Rumford, the Life and Public Services of a California Legislator: A Biography.* El Cerrito: Downey Place, 1974.

East Bay Regional Park District. Archive, scrapbooks.

Ferrier, William Warren. *Berkeley California: The Story of the Evolution of a Hamlet into a City of Culture and Commerce.* Berkeley: self-published, 1933.

———. *Henry Durant, First President University of California: The New Englander Who Came to California with College on the Brain.* Berkeley: self-published, 1942.

Herken, Gregg. *Brotherhood of the Bomb: the Tangled Lives and Loyalties of Robert Oppenheimer, Ernest Lawrence, and Edward Teller.* New York: Henry Holt, 2002.

Herny, Ed, Shelley Rideout, and Katie Wadell. *Berkeley Bohemia.* Berkeley: Berkeley Historical Society, 2007.

Hudson, Marsha. *The Berkeley Literary Women's Revolution: Essays from Marsha's Salon.* Jefferson, NC: McFarland & Co., 2005.

Hughes, Robert A. "Making a House a Home: 70 Years of Student Co-ops." *California Monthly*, November 2003.

Hume, Samuel, and Portia Bell Hume. Papers. Bancroft Library, University of California, Berkeley.

Hussey, Marguerite C. *Recollections of Life in Northeast Berkeley, 1859–1910.* An oral history transcript with Louis Stein Jr. conducted in 1981 by Karen Jorgensen-Esmaili for the Oral History Committee, Berkeley Architectural Heritage Association and Berkeley Historical Society, 1982.

Jones, William Carey. *Illustrated History of the University of California.* Berkeley: Students' Cooperative Society, 1901.

Keeler, Charles. Papers. Bancroft Library, University of California, Berkeley.

———. *An Epitome of Cosmic Religion.* Berkeley: The Sign of the Live Oak, 1925.

Keith, William, Mary McHenry Keith, and others. Keith-McHenry-Pond family papers. Bancroft Library, University of California, Berkeley.

Kingman, Harry L. Papers, 1921–1975. Bancroft Library, University of California, Berkeley.

Lee, Warren F. *A Selective History of the Codornices-University Village, the City of Albany and Environs.* Albuquerque, NM: self-published, 2000.

Lillian, Guy H. *Cheap Place to Live.* Manuscript at Berkeley Historical Society, no date.

Margolin, Malcolm. *The Ohlone Way.* Berkeley: Heyday Books, 1978.

May, Henry Farnham. *The Three Faces of Berkeley: Competing Ideologies in the Wheeler Era.* Berkeley: Center for Studies in Higher Education and Institute of Governmental Studies, 1993.

Maybeck, Bernard, and Annie Maybeck. Bernard and Annie Maybeck, transcript of a KPFA interview conducted by Bob Schutz, 1952–53. Berkeley Historical Society, Berkeley.

Maybeck, Jacomena. *Maybeck: The Family View.* Berkeley: Berkeley Architectural Heritage Association, 1980.

McArdle, Phil, ed. *Exactly Opposite the Golden Gate: Essays on Berkeley's History.* Berkeley: Berkeley Historical Society, 1983.

Nathan, Harriet, and Stanley Scott, eds. *Experiment and Change in Berkeley: Essays on City Politics, 1950–1975.* Berkeley: Institute of Governmental Studies, UC Berkeley, 1978.

Neptune, Robert. A conversation with Robert Neptune, pioneer manager of the Consumers Cooperative of Berkeley and long-term manager at Associated Cooperatives. Oral history conducted by Therese Pipe, 1996. Berkeley Oral History Project of the Berkeley Historical Society.

Neuhaus, Eugen. *William Keith, the Man and the Artist*, Berkeley: University of California Press, 1938.

———. *Reminiscences: Bay Area Art and the University of California Art Department*. Oral history transcript onducted by Suzanne B. Riess. Regional Cultural History Project, University of California, Berkeley, 1961.

Olmsted Brothers and Ansel F. Hall. *Report on Proposed Park Reservations for East Bay Cities*, 1930. Reprinted 1984.

Partin, Agnes Edwards. Edited by Grace E. Moremen. *Student Life at the University of California, Berkeley During and After World War I*. Lewiston, New York: Edwin Mellen Press, 2006.

Pettitt, George. *Berkeley: The Town and Gown of It*. Berkeley: Howell-North Books, 1973.

Pitcher, Don, *Berkeley Inside/Out*. Berkeley: Heyday Books, 1989.

Richardson, Leon Josiah. *Berkeley Culture, University of California Highlights, and University Extension, 1892–1960*. Oral history transcript conducted by Amelia R. Fry. Regional Cultural History Project, University of California, Berkeley.

Save San Francisco Bay Association, 1961–1986. Oral history transcript, Regional Oral History Office of the University of California, Bancroft Library. Interviews conducted by Malca Chall.

Schwartz, Richard. *Berkeley 1900: Daily Life at the Turn of the Century*. Berkeley: RBS Books, 2000.

———. *Earthquake Exodus, 1906*. Berkeley: RBS Books, 2005.

Sibley, Carol. *Building Community Trust, Berkeley School Integration and other Civic Endeavors, 1943–1978*. Oral history transcript, Regional Oral History Office of the University of California, Bancroft Library, 1978.

Sibley, Robert. Papers, 1881–1958. Bancroft Library, University of California, Berkeley.

Stadtman, Verne. *The University of California, 1868–1969*. New York: McGraw-Hill, 1970.

Stewart, George. *The Year of the Oath: The Fight for Academic Freedom at the University of California*. New York: Da Capo Press, 1971.

Warshaw, Steven. *The Trouble in Berkeley: The Complete History, in Text and Pictures, of the Great Student Rebellion Against the "New University."* Berkeley: Diablo Press, 1965.

Willes, Burl. *Picturing Berkeley: A Postcard History*. Salt Lake City: Gibbs Smith, 2002.

———. *Quick Index to the Origin of Berkeley's Names*. Berkeley: Berkeley Historical Society, 2004.

Willey, S. H. "The College of California." *Overland Monthly*, July 1885.

Wollenberg, Charles. *Berkeley: A City in History*. Berkeley: University of California Press, 2008.

Woodbridge, Salley. *John Galen Howard and the University of California: The Design of a Great Public University Campus*. Berkeley: University of California Press, 2002.

Yamada, Robert. *The Japanese American Experience: The Berkeley Legacy*. Berkeley: Berkeley Historical Society, 1995.

Index

Dave Weinstein,

also wrote Signature Architects of the San Francisco Bay Area *and the text for* Berkeley Rocks: Building with Nature. *He writes about historic architecture for the* San Francisco Chronicle *and about modern architecture for* CA Modern *magazine. He is chairman of the Friends of the Cerrito Theater.*

IT CAME FRO